Sto

9-5-61

POETS AND STORY-TELLERS

DAVID CECIL

POETS
AND STORY-TELLERS

New York

BARNES & NOBLE INC.

PRINTED IN GREAT BRITAIN BY
LOWE AND BRYDONE (PRINTERS) LIMITED, LONDON, N.W.10

1167746

PREFATORY NOTE

My thanks are due to the Oxford University Press, the Cambridge University Press, Geoffrey Cumberlege, Jackson Son & Company, and *The Listener* for permission to reprint essays in this volume.

"Antony and Cleopatra" was the fourth W. P. Ker Memorial Lecture delivered in the University of Glasgow in 1943; "Thomas Gray" was the subject of the Warton Lecture on English poetry delivered to the British Academy in 1945; and "Jane Austen" was the Leslie Stephen Lecture delivered in the University of Cambridge in 1935.

"A genuine criticism should, as I take it, reflect the colours, the light and shade, the soul and body of a work . . . what the essence of the work is, what passion has been touched or how skilfully, what tone and movement the author's mind imparts to his subject or receives from it."

WILLIAM HAZLITT

"The function of the aesthetic critic is to distinguish, to analyse, and separate from its adjuncts, the virtue by which a picture, a landscape, a fair personality in life or in a book, produces this special impression of beauty or pleasure, to indicate what the source of that impression is, and under what conditions it is experienced. . . . He will remember always that beauty exists in many forms. To him all periods, types, schools of taste, are in themselves equal. In all ages there have been some excellent workmen, and some excellent work done."

WALTER PATER

CONTENTS

"ANTONY AND CLEOPATRA"

"ANTONY AND CLEOPATRA" has been discussed by all sorts of eminent persons from Coleridge downwards. Yet its position in Shakespeare's work has remained ambiguous. You have only to read the comments on it to realise this. Their authors all speak of it as one of Shakespeare's greatest performances: they all agree that it contains some of his most magnificent work. But, in the midst of their pæans of praise, they suddenly let fall a sentence which shows that their feelings about it are divided, that they do not quite know what to make of it. Here is Professor Dowden, for instance, who finds huge chunks of it irrelevant to the main theme. Can it be a reversion, he suggests, to Shakespeare's earlier historical manner, when he just dramatised a chronicle as it came, without troubling to shape it into a pattern? Bradley thinks its whole middle section deficient in dramatic tension. He also finds the moral atmosphere unpleasant, lacking in nobility compared with Shakespeare's greatest tragedies. While as for Dr. Johnson he is openly scandalised by the heroine's deplorable lack of dignity. The arts of Cleopatra, he asserts majestically, are too low.

These are grave accusations. How can a play be a masterpiece which is badly constructed, padded out with irrelevant matter, and in which the heroine's behaviour is shockingly "low"? Even if it contains splendid passages, it must, considered as a whole, be judged an unsatisfactory piece of work. But, in fact, is this the impression that it does leave on anyone who comes to it with a mind unprejudiced by the carpings of the critics? Surely not! The reader, if he surrenders himself to the play's spell, finds himself borne steadily onwards at a height of unqualified delight. He does not mind the so-called irrelevancy, he rejoices at the spectacle of Cleopatra's arts at work, he feels no relaxation of tension anywhere in the play. The impression left in his memory is of a harmonious radiance in the light of which all these criticisms appear off the point. And, as a matter of fact, that is what they are. They are made because their authors have fallen into the most common error of criticism; condemning a work for failing to be something it was never intended to be.

We can see how they have gone wrong. The play deals with a famous love-story; and it is to be found in that section of Shakespeare's dramas devoted to his tragedies. Critics therefore assume that it is a tragic drama like the others; and that its theme is love. Now, if this were true, there is no doubt it would be full of faults. Apart from anything else, much of it is not dramatic at all, in the sense that *Othello* is dramatic. Consider the first two acts. The scene switches capriciously about. Now we are in Egypt listening to court ladies jesting and gossiping, now in Rome among wrangling statesmen, now in Sicily witnessing a drunken party. Numbers of characters cross the stage, talking a lot and doing very little. There are quarrels and reconciliations; people start a campaign and give it up; suddenly a marriage is arranged. No one seems to feel very strongly about anything or to pursue any line of action consistently. After the first two acts the action does begin to develop. But it repeats itself a good deal.

Antony quarrels with Cleopatra, then forgives her. They both fly from Caesar, then make a stand, then fly again. Meanwhile, several of the figures, Pompey for example, who have an important part in the early section of the play, have vanished from the scene without explanation.

Nor is *Antony and Cleopatra* tragic, as *King Lear* is tragic. It is only when the story gets going in the third act that emotion rises to tragic intensity; the first part is diversified by a number of satirical and comic scenes. The hero and heroine themselves are often the objects of satire. Antony gets drunk: Cleopatra slaps her servant in an absurd explosion of petty feminine jealousy. We do not find Othello or Lady Macbeth behaving in this undignified fashion, reprehensible as their characters are in many respects. Finally, if love is meant to be the main theme, Shakespeare is shockingly careless about sticking to it. A large part of the plot has nothing to do with the love-story. No light is thrown on the relations of Antony and Cleopatra by the scenes about Pompey's rebellion. When that is over, just when we think we are getting back to the love-story again, we find ourselves transported to Parthia where we are made to listen to one of Antony's lieutenants Ventidius commenting on how the news of his success in battle will be received by the government. No—if *Antony and Cleopatra* is meant to be a typical Shakesperean tragic drama, with love as its theme, it is a failure. But we enjoy it: and one does not enjoy failures. Perhaps these neat categories of tragedy and love story do not apply to it.

Indeed, such categories seldom do apply to Shakespeare's plays—or for that matter to those of any

Elizabethan dramatist. People do not always realise what an irregular haphazard affair the Elizabethan drama was. It was so new for one thing; it only came into being thirty odd years before Shakespeare appeared. And like Shakespeare himself, it began in very humble circumstances. Troops of vagabond mummers set up a rough theatre in which they made a precarious living by providing entertainment for any audience they could persuade to listen to them. The audience moreover, was unsophisticated. It had no theories as to what drama ought to be. All it wanted was to be entertained: and its taste in entertainment was greedy, child-like and sensational. The aim of the dramatist was to pack into two short hours every element of entertainment that could appeal to such an audience; realism and phantasy, farce and melodrama, prose and poetry, jokes and horrors, glamorous fairy-tale characters, and coarse topical witticisms, all jumbled together in one highly-coloured hotch-potch. The dramatist had no rules or tradition of art to work on. As long as he gave pleasure he could do what he liked.

This was not an advantage to most writers. Most writers, like most men, are not strong enough to bear complete liberty. Shakespeare was the one exception. He not only triumphed over the defects of his form. He turned them into assets. He was not a revolutionary. His plays are composed of the same jumble of heterogeneous elements as are those of his fellows. But his sense of design was so powerful that he was able to impose an order on them; and he used the freedom allowed to him to create a richer and more diverse picture of life than could have been included in a

stricter form. There is no formula for a Shakespeare
play. He does anything he likes, changes the scene,
varies the characters, digresses from the main theme,
is comic or tragic, or poetic just as it suits his conception
of his story. Nor does he mould his plot into any
accepted pattern of correct play-making. If we are to
appreciate him properly therefore, we must free our
minds from any pre-conceived ideas of what drama
ought to be. For he observes no laws other than those
which his taste dictates to suit each particular subject
he chooses. This is true of all his plays. But in none
is he so audaciously lawless as in *Antony and Cleopatra*. It
is the most virtuosic of all his performances; that in
which, arrived as he was at the full maturity of his
superb technical accomplishment, he stretches the
capacities of his form to the most daring limits. Never
was he so dazzlingly original, either in conception or
execution. No wonder that orthodox critics have been
bewildered; no wonder they are worried that it fails
to fit into any of their categories of tragedy or love-story
or drama. For it is none of these things. It is the single
unique example of its species.

Let us examine the story which was his source;
and then see what he made of it. The story of Antony
and Cleopatra as related by Plutarch begins shortly
after the defeat of Julius Caesar's murderers. Antony
and Octavius Caesar are left candidates for the mastery
of the Roman world. The chances between them seemed
very even. But, just as Antony should have been
exerting all his powers to obtain the prize, he met
Cleopatra, and fell in love with her. Absorbed in the
enjoyment of her charms he began to let power slip
from his fingers. Disturbances started to break out all

B

over the Empire. If Antony did not exert himself, it was clear that Octavius or some other man, possibly Pompey, would outdistance him. Antony broke away from Cleopatra, allied with Octavius, sealed the reconciliation by marrying Octavius's sister, and forced Pompey to make peace. But the memory of Cleopatra's charms was too much for him, and he returned to her. Octavius took advantage of this excuse to attack Antony, who, misled by the influence of Cleopatra, first challenged Octavius to fight at sea, where he, Antony, was weakest; and, when she fled in the middle of the battle, fled after her. For a little, he fought a spasmodic ineffective rearguard action; then, realising all was lost, killed himself. Cleopatra fell into Octavius's hands; but only to follow her lover's example a few days later.

Now, how does Shakespeare attack this heap of complex historical material with a view to extracting a single coherent drama from it? It is all nonsense, I may say in passing, to suggest that he dramatised the story just as it came, in chronicle fashion. He leaves a lot of Plutarch out, and what he leaves in, he often alters. Clearly, there is a deliberate purpose behind his treatment. What was it? The first thing to be said about it is that it is different from that of any other writer—there are a great many of them—who has tried to make a play out of the same story. These others concentrated exclusively on the love-story. Not so Shakespeare. With him the love-story is seen always in its relation to the rivalry between Octavius and Antony. A large part of the play is concerned with this only, and not with the love-story at all. We see Antony with Octavius and Pompey and his soldiers quite as

much as we see him with Cleopatra. We also see
Pompey, Octavius and the soldiers by themselves,
without Antony. Shakespeare conceives his play as a
piece of history; its interest is largely political.

In this it is of a piece with his other Roman plays.
The Roman tragedies differ from the other tragedies,
in that they are concerned, not so much with man's
private inner life, as with his life in the theatre of
public affairs. *Macbeth* and *Coriolanus* both deal with a
struggle for government. But, whereas in *Macbeth* our
attention is directed to the conflict between the hero's
ambition and his conscience, in *Coriolanus* it is directed
to the conflict between the hero and the people of
Rome. The Roman plays deal with human beings;
but human beings in their external and political aspect,
with the clash of character in action on the public
stage. Not which side of the hero's nature will prevail,
but which person or group of persons will prevail in the
political struggle, is the issue presented for our attention.
Coriolanus is pitted against the people of Rome;
Julius Caesar's murderers are pitted against Octavius
and Antony. In these plays the public nature of the
drama is obvious. It is not so obvious in *Antony and
Cleopatra*. Here there is more private life. But the
private life is, as it were, a consequence of the public
life. *Antony and Cleopatra* completes the story begun in
Julius Caesar. The end of *Julius Caesar* left Octavius
and Antony sole rivals for the mastery of the Roman
Empire after their victory over Brutus and Cassius.
Naturally they come into conflict. This conflict between
them dictates the general lines on which Shakespeare's
play is designed. But history relates that Antony was
defeated in it because of his love for Cleopatra. Now

this brings in a new element. Love is an extremely private emotion. If Shakespeare means to do justice to it he must leave the theatre of public life during a large part of his play. All the same the love-story is only one feature in a bigger picture. Always as Shakespeare saw it, it is related to the public drama, and is inseparably connected with it. Its nature would be essentially altered were it to be transferred to a private setting. If Antony and Cleopatra had been private persons, their story simply could not have happened.

His public character is further emphasised by the fashion in which Shakespeare conceives his characters. They are people of action, not thinkers or philosophers. They never withdraw, like Hamlet, to contemplate their story from a detached point of view; and to draw conclusions from it about human life in general. Octavius may let fall a sentence about the inevitability of fate: "But let determined things to destiny hold unbewailed their way." Having said this, however, he continues his career of crafty political scheming. Neither he nor anyone else questions the value of the sort of life they live. Antony, it is true, sacrifices his power to his love for Cleopatra. But he does not do it deliberately. He is so besotted with Cleopatra he cannot give her up; and he deludes himself into thinking that he can somehow manage to have her and political power at once. The very splendour and spaciousness of his mode of life narrowed his vision as it narrows that of his rival. Set high on the throne of the whole known world, the awe and admiration of mankind, they do not doubt that the world's standards are the right standards.

Further, they do not think it right to disregard the impression that their behaviour makes on others. Always they are influenced by the consciousness that they are public persons. Even in the final catastrophe of the play, Antony feels himself driven to suicide, partly because he believes Cleopatra to have killed herself, and he cannot bear to live without her, but still more because she has shewn him the right way for a great man to conduct himself before the world in disaster. With his last breath he expresses his pride that he has been able to do this.

> The miserable change now at my end
> Lament nor sorrow at; but please your thoughts
> In feeding them with those my former fortunes
> Wherein I liv'd, the greatest prince o' the world,
> The noblest; and do now not basely die,
> Not cowardly put off my helmet to
> My countryman; a Roman by a Roman
> Valiantly vanquish'd. Now my spirit is going;
> I can no more.

Cleopatra is still more dominated by the thought of the figure she cuts. She resolves to kill herself when Antony dies; but she cannot bring herself to do it till she realises that otherwise she will be led publicly in triumph through the streets of Rome. No doubt this is lamentable evidence of her vanity, as her severely-principled critics have not failed to point out. Antony too is vain. But their regard for their reputations is not due only to ignoble motives. It is the inevitable consequence of the light in which they regarded their own position. They are what the Elizabethan calls "great persons"; it was the duty of great persons to behave as such, to take into consideration when deciding on a course of action the impression it would make on the huge audience before whom their lives were acted out. The play is about Kings and Queens and Emperors. They realise it themselves; and Shakespeare means us to realise it too.

Not that it is a play about kingship or imperialism. Shakespeare, as far as we can tell from his work, was not interested in abstract principles. Politics to him meant politicians. History, as he saw it, was the history of individual human beings. The fact that Cleopatra was a queen interested Shakespeare only in so far as it modified her personal character. The clash between Antony and Octavius stirs his attention not as the clash between two different causes, but as the clash between two different sorts of men. He is always striving to penetrate through his characters' official personalities to find the human being. We see the drama of the great world behind the scenes. And "Look", Shakespeare seems to say to us, "look, I will show you what these famous people, whom you only see from a distance, seem like close at hand; this is the sort of life they lead —this is the sort of motive that actuates them." *Antony and Cleopatra* is a study in the life of the great political world, as it shewed itself to one interested in individual human nature. Incidentally, the story must have seemed far more realistic and topical in Shakespeare's day than now. In a monarchial and courtly age, personality and personal feeling counted for a great deal in politics. The personal rivalry of Charles V and Francis I had caused a European war: the personal passions of Henry VIII had brought about the English Reformation. Women indeed, it is to be noted, influenced public affairs more decisively when they entered them as queens than as lady members of parliament. Shakespeare remembered Queen Elizabeth and Catherine de Medici and Mary, Queen of Scots. There is of course no question of *Antony and Cleopatra* being a play about contemporary events under an historical guise. But it can be taken that Shakespeare's omnivorous curiosity was directed at this time to the great world of public affairs; and that this play is the result of his cogitations on the subject.

The character of his picture is further determined by the interpretation he puts on Plutarch's story. To Shakespeare this story was inevitably predestined. Here again his version is different from that given by other writers. These presented it as turning on an uncertain conflict between Antony's love and his political ambition. Antony could have chosen to give up Cleopatra; if he had, he would then have overcome Octavius. As Shakespeare saw the matter there was no question of this. Antony's character made it impossible. He is presented as a typical Elizabethan "great man", brilliant and confident, audacious and unscrupulous, a brave soldier, a subtle diplomat, and with that personal magnetism that, without effort, compels the hearts of his followers. Even cynical Enobarbus loves him; when he publicly bids farewell to his soldiers, he brings tears to every eye. Was he not the same Antony that had won over the people of Rome, after the murder of Caesar, by a single speech? But the very fact that he could achieve success so easily had stopped him from ever learning self-discipline. He is a profoundly self-indulgent character. Trusting to his natural gifts to

carry him through a crisis, he had never taught himself
to subdue an immediate desire in order to achieve a
further end; with the result that he always evaded
making the decision between the claims of his public
career and his private feelings. He might leave
Cleopatra for a time, when things looked bad. But
when they looked better again and he began to grow
bored, back he went to her. Surely, he told himself, a
man of his personality could keep his power and
Cleopatra as well. Gradually this habit of mind grew
so strong that he gave in to it even when his wiser self
had begun to suspect that the issue was not so certain.
He fights at sea against his better judgment just because
she wants him to; when she flees from the battle, he
follows her. It was not that love blinds him to her true
character. He realises only too well that she was so
unstable that he could not trust her to be consistently
loyal to her love for him, let alone to give a sound
impartial political judgment. But he had yielded to
her so often that now he was incapable of putting up
any resistance, however important the issue. The odds
against him were further lengthened by the fact that
Octavius, as Shakespeare conceived him, was just the
opposite kind of man, far-sighted, cool, self-controlled,
and so single-mindedly intent on the achievement of
his ambition, that nothing, neither the happiness of his
sister nor a genuine feeling of pity for Antony in his fall,
can turn him from it. When, at the end, Cleopatra
tries her charms on Octavius, he appreciates them—
"her strong toil of grace" he speaks of—but he does not
succumb to them for an instant. If such are the
elements in the situation, its outcome is clear. Octavius
must defeat Antony.

But there are hints that Shakespeare looked on his end as determined by greater forces even than these innate qualities of the actors. Early in the play into the frivolous worldly atmosphere of Court and Council Chamber he introduces the strange figure of the soothsayer. Ostensibly he is only a tame fortune-teller hanging about the Court for the entertainment of idle people. Nobody seems to take his predictions very seriously. They are wrong. When Cleopatra's ladies ask him about their future, in occult terms the sooth-sayer foretells their dreadful end. And when Antony casually asks him whether he or Octavius is likely to get the better of the other, he replies:

... stay not by his side;
Thy demon—that's thy spirit which keeps thee,—is
Noble, courageous, high, unmatchable,
Where Caesar's is not; but near him thy angel
Becomes a fear, as being o'erpowered; therefore
Make space enough between you.

ANTHONY.   Speak this no more.
SOOTHSAYER. To none but thee; no more but when
    to thee.
If thou dost play with him at any game
Thou art sure to lose, and, of that natural luck,
He beats thee 'gainst the odds; thy lustre thickens
When he shines by. I say again, thy spirit
Is all afraid to govern thee near him,
But he away, 'tis noble.

Destiny, so Shakespeare suggests, a supernatural destiny is working behind the visible scene to promote its secret purpose. These great persons, apparently so powerful, and with the world at their feet, are in reality no more than puppets in the fingers of a mysterious and irresistible fate. The personal drama is seen as part of a huge impersonal historical process.

It is, surely, an unusual subject for a play—a wedge of political history in which every event is represented as inevitable. Shakespeare invents a very unusual form to fit it. He takes every advantage of the freedom allowed to an Elizabethan dramatist. There is not a rule of conventional play-making he does not break. For one thing, he begins the story in the middle. The ordinary dramatist would have started with the meeting of Antony and Cleopatra, and worked it up to a dramatic crisis, in which Antony would decide between his love and his ambition. The last section of the play would relate the consequences of this decision. Such a plan does not fit Shakespeare's interpretation of the story. He therefore begins when Antony, already caught up in Cleopatra's toils, first suspects that his political position is endangered. He goes back to Rome, makes it up with Octavius, and marries Octavia, but decides all the same to return to Cleopatra. This is the first section of the play. When the third act begins he is back in Egypt; and Octavius has already broken with him. The rest of the play traces in detail the gradual process of Octavius's victory. But there is no rise and fall of the hero's fortunes. The play opens with Antony poised at the top of a slope as it were. After a little uncertainty, he begins to slide down, and then proceeds faster and faster until he reaches the bottom. The play would have been better entitled "*The Decline and Fall of Antony*". Shakespeare deliberately renounces the possibilities of dramatic suspense offered by the plot. Moreover, so far from keeping out in the dark as to what is going to happen, he forewarns us of it in the second act. When Antony has broken with Cleopatra, Shakespeare goes out of his way to introduce a scene in which Enobarbus states that this breach is not likely to be a final one.

> MECAENAS. Now Antony must leave her utterly.
> ENOBARBUS. Never; he will not:
> Age cannot wither her, nor custom stale
> Her infinite variety; . . .

The Soothsayer, too, explains that Octavius is fated always to overcome him. Antony's rivalry with Octavius and his love for Cleopatra—these are the two questions with which the plot is concerned; and the answers to both are made clear from the first. That both Cleopatra and Octavius will prevail is presented to us as axiomatic: we are meant to start off taking them for granted. Shakespeare is so little interested in the more obvious dramatic possibilities of the story, that he does not even make the most of any crisis that does occur in his version of it. There are three turning points in the action of the first two acts. Antony leaves Egypt to go to Rome; he comes back to Cleopatra; Octavius breaks with him. The first of these, his farewell to Cleopatra, is presented deliberately in a light vein, without any heightening of the dramatic tension; neither of the other two takes place on the stage at all. We are told about them, after they have happened. As Shakespeare sees it, what happened is too obvious to be interesting. He is concerned with how it happened. He wishes to show the effect of events on character, to trace in what way their declining fortunes gradually affected Antony, Cleopatra, and their followers. Always we see the actors close up, before critical events take place, and afterwards; Antony before he leaves Egypt, and after he returns to it; Octavius before he breaks with Antony and after the breach. Only at the last, when events are rising to their final climax, does decisive action take place on the stage. The drama of the decline and fall of Antony groups itself into three sections. In the first two acts the situation is expounded to us, in the third and part of the fourth we follow the process of decline, and still more its effect on the actors. The last section exhibits in detail the incidents of that catastrophe which is the logical outcome of all that has gone before.

The form of the play is further conditioned by the fact that Shakespeare envisages it as a piece of history. Since it is a play about the great world of affairs, this great world must be kept in view. In order to do this, Shakespeare again makes use of the Elizabethan freedom. He moves the scene about all over the Roman world. Now we are in Rome, now we are in Egypt, now in Sicily; for a moment we are wafted to Parthia. With diversity of scene goes diversity of character. The stage is crowded with those humbler persons whose fortunes depend on those of the principal actors— courtiers, soldiers, councillors. Never once do the lovers appear alone with each other. Round them hover Antony's staff, Cleopatra's ladies and eunuchs. We are constantly kept in mind of the public nature of the subject; we are never intended to forget that Antony's defeat will prove a disaster to all who have ranged themselves under his banner. And we see both him and Cleopatra as they appear to the world. When the great persons leave the scene, the lesser ones stay behind and make their cynical or enthusiastic comments on them.

This historical attitude to his subject is also responsible for the fact that the play is so much more varied in mood than are Shakespeare's regular tragedies. A convincing picture of the great world cannot be steeped in the consistently tragic atmosphere which envelops *King Lear*. To a detached observer, the life of the great world is never consistently tragic; it is an extraordinary compound of sad and comic, prosaic and poetic. So is Shakespeare's play. There is a great deal of comedy in it; ranging from the farcical humour of the clown, who brings the means of death to Cleopatra—ironically this illustrates how little the great and their misfortunes mean to the humble—to the cool satire of the scene on Pompey's galley, when "the third part of the world" is carried drunk to bed. For these great people, as Shakespeare sees them, are far from being as dignified as they wish to appear. Cleopatra herself, during the first half of the play, is a comedy figure, with her petty feminine vanity, her childish lack of self-control. Even at the end, when she is on the point of killing herself, she cuffs her treasurer in a fit of temper because he gives away the fact that she has been trying to deceive Octavius as to the real amount of her treasure. Yet, mingled with all this comedy is the grave statesman's wisdom of the political drama, the tragic pathos of Enobarbus' end, the passionate lyrical beauty of the love scenes, the supernatural mystery of the soothsayer scenes, or that in which the soldiers hear the fading unearthly music which betokens the departure of the god Hercules, who had, up to then, protected Antony's fortunes; while over all glows the light of Shakespeare's sense of the romance inherent in grand historic events.

Looked at from the right angle then, those features of Shakespeare's play which have bewildered his critics appear clear and explicable. They are the logical consequence of the way in which he sees his subject. He envisages it less as a drama than as a panorama. Yet, to recognise this is not to prove the critics wrong in their feeling of dissatisfaction. After all, *Antony and Cleopatra* sets out to be a work of art; and a panorama and a work of art are not the same thing. A work of art must have unity, pattern, significance; a panorama need have none of these things. It is Shakespeare's triumph that he does manage to make his panorama into a work of art. For the incoherent heterogeneous material which is his subject-matter is all made to relate to a single presiding theme. This theme is not love; it is success. This fact is the master-key to the riddle of the play. Shakespeare looks at the chaotic spectacle of the great world convulsed in the struggle for power and happiness; and, he asks "What sort of man is successful in it?" Seen in relation to this steady canon of judgment, all the confused variety of his subject falls into proportion and significance. Shakespeare puts his question from various points of view. First of all, he asks, "Which candidate is likely to gain command of the Roman Empire?" Lepidus? No!—he is a weak fool. Pompey? No!—too scrupulous or too timid, he refuses his one chance of getting rid of his competitors when he has them at his mercy. The

real test is between Antony and Octavius, Antony the
gifted, instinctive, leader of men, or Octavius, the
prudent, far-sighted statesman. There is no doubt
about Shakespeare's answer. For good or for ill, it is
the Octaviuses who get their way in this world.

But Shakespeare does not stop here. To so profound
a mind as his, the achievement of worldly power cannot be a final test of success. He goes on to ask, "Is
worldly success really worth having?" Shakespeare's
unillusioned examination of the story has made him
very doubtful. A profound irony colours the scene.
Certainly worldly success is not necessarily a proof of
worthy service. This is the lesson taught us by the odd
little scene in Parthia. Ventidius it is, who is doing
Rome real service by defeating her enemies. But he is
not a candidate for the throne. On the contrary, he is
only too well aware that his very victories may do his
career harm, by arousing the jealousy of his master.
Again, to sacrifice all to worldly considerations may
involve the loss of happiness. Consider the case of
Enobarbus. He serves Antony loyally as long as he
thinks Antony has a chance of victory. But when he
deliberately throws this away from self-indulgent
motives, Enobarbus feels justified in leaving him. He
cannot be blamed; but, in the event, it proves a terrible
mistake. For he loves Antony. Tortured by what he
feels to be his treachery, he dies of a broken heart.

But the crucial issue is, of course, that exhibited by
Antony's own story. Was he right or wrong in yielding
to love rather than to political ambition? Shakespeare
is rigorously impartial on the subject. The world of
public life is not shewn to us in an ideal light. On the
contrary, it is a seething whirlpool of competition and

intrigue in which everyone is more or less unscrupulous and no one is wholly disinterested. Antony and Caesar alike are actuated less by a sense of duty, than by the desire to cut a great figure in the world. Yet Shakespeare's attitude is not wholly unsympathetic. For he shared the Elizabethan belief in personal greatness. He thought it natural to want to cut a figure. Like Tamburlaine, he felt it was brave to be a king and ride in triumph through Persepolis. Moreover Antony and Caesar are superior spirits. Shakespeare believed that a superior spirit rightly desires dominion and magnificence. The love-story is presented in an equally impartial way. Neither Antony nor Cleopatra is an ideal figure. They are both middle-aged. Antony's love is a self-indulgent passion that weakens his will and blinds his judgment. While Cleopatra is, by a strict moral standard, a vain, worthless, capricious coquette who does not care in the least about the true interests of her lover, and who is so dominated by the desire to attract that she cannot be faithful to him for half-an-hour once his back is turned. Yet in spite of all, the figures of both are resplendent with romance. Antony is a true king of men, with his charm and his generosity, his courage and rich vein of poetry. As for Cleopatra, she is simply the sorceress of the world. Who could resist such vitality, such grace, such temperament, such wit, so exquisite and unquenchable a sense of pleasure? And their love—how insipid most passions appear in comparison with this leaping, burning, many-coloured fire, aromatic with all the imperial seductiveness of Shakespeare's mature poetic style. Such a love for such a woman is worth weighing in the balance against the empire of the whole known world.

"The nobleness of life is to do thus," says Antony as he kisses her. Are we so sure he is wrong?

Thus Shakespeare states his problem. But himself he gives no answer. Olympian, and enigmatic, he presents us with the evidence and leaves us to judge. It is this ambiguity, I suspect, which has, in reality, given the critics their feeling of dissatisfaction. People often think themselves displeased with a work of art when, in fact, they are displeased with the man who created it. Critics, most of them, are moralists who judge, first of all, by standards of right and wrong. Artists often are not. Artists seldom are the same sort of people as critics—that is why so much criticism is inept. Shakespeare was not a moralist. He appreciated goodness, and disliked evil; but he did not approach life primarily from the moral point of view. He was an observer, and an aesthete. Life interested him passionately: and what stirred him most in it was its beauty, its delightfulness, its power to appeal to the senses, the heart, the imagination. Observation made him unillusioned; appreciation made him romantic; disillusionment and sense of romance combined in an ironical zest for the spectacle of the world, often incompatible with a decisive moral judgment. Some of his most memorable characters—those in which we feel he is expressing his most fundamental sense of values—leave the reader's moral judgment somehow in suspense. Falstaff for instance—is he an old ruffian rightly cast off by the virtuous young King? Or a rollicking enchanting incarnation of the joy of life, rejected by a cold-hearted prig? Shakespeare does not say. Richard II too—is he too fine a spirit to be successful in a coarse and humdrum world? Or a

c

weak sentimentalist justly brought to disaster? Shakespeare leaves it to us to decide. And Hamlet himself;
does he fail to carry out the ghost's commands because
he is too weak or because he is too wise? Shakespeare
does not tell us what he thinks. So it is with Antony.
Mr. Bernard Shaw thinks he is a sternly realistic
portrait of a man who destroyed his life by self-
indulgence. Others have seen in him a glorious example
of one who is prepared to sacrifice all for love. I do
not think either is right. They achieve their certainty
only by shutting their eyes to one aspect of the truth.
Shakespeare is more candid. He states all the facts.
And his conclusion seems to be that it is impossible to
be certain in our judgment of Antony's conduct.

The moralistic critic finds such uncertainty painful.
To him, a world in which he cannot be sure whom to
praise, whom to blame is a disheartening place, whose
apparent glories must be suspect. But Shakespeare is
only disheartened by a world without glory, a world
which weakens his gusto for living. In his darkest
mood, he has shown us such a world. But this is not
the mood which informs *Antony and Cleopatra*. On the
contrary, in it Shakespeare teaches us that it is possible
to face life at its most baffling and imperfect and unideal,
and yet to find it inextinguishably enthralling and
splendid. It is a lesson well worth learning.

JOHN WEBSTER

JOHN WEBSTER

JOHN WEBSTER, in one of the few personal utterances of his that have come down to us, complained that his work was not valued at its true worth. And the history of his reputation supports his view. Moderately admired during his lifetime, he fell for 200 years almost into oblivion. With the romantic movement, however, the tide turned. Webster was singled out for commendation by a succession of distinguished critics; Lamb, Swinburne, Rupert Brooke. Gradually their words had effect. Webster was more and more read, discussed and praised till during the last two years his two most famous plays have been put on with some success for ordinary runs in the commercial London theatre; an honour shared by no other Elizabethan tragedian except Shakespeare. All the same it is doubtful if he has yet been properly appreciated. Even those who have been most enthusiastic about him have not truly grasped the nature of his achievement. He is generally talked about as an instinctive barbarous genius, the author of a pair of bloody, incoherent melodramas, saved from absurdity by magnificence of language and the intensity of individual scenes. It is easy to see why they have made this impression. The Elizabethan drama—unlike most great drama—was not a civilised form of art designed to gratify a fastidious trained taste. It was a popular entertainment, whose first aim was to give immediate pleasure to a mixed audience, whose

taste was, in many respects, crude and childish. The
Elizabethans did not demand from their dramatists
logical consistency, or probability or restraint. What
they wanted was sensation; an exciting plot, in
which grand and glamorous personages went through
the most extraordinary vicissitudes of fortune, involving
as many murders and suicides and ghosts and lunatics
and scenes of torture or pageantry as could be crammed
into two hours. Most of their playwrights gave them
these things—with the addition of some passages of
eloquent verse. And they gave them nothing more.

At first glance Webster seems just the same as his
fellows. No plays contain more ghosts and lunatics and
massacres than his; and no plots, by any realistic
standard, are more irrational. Why should Ludovico
in *The White Devil* be devoting his whole life, at
appalling risk to himself, to avenging the Duchess
Isabella whom he hardly knew? Why should the
Duchess of Malfi's two brothers object so violently to
her second marriage, if she already had an heir to take
the inheritance from them? And why, incidentally
should they delay for the two or three years necessary
for her to have produced three children, before taking
the vengeance on her? Nor are Webster's stories made
more convincing by the fact that he will digress from
the main action to bring in long scenes of irrelevant
pageantry like those of the Pope's election in *The White
Devil*. Certainly he does not seem a serious and deliberate artist.

However he himself thought he was. In the preface
to *The White Devil* he speaks of his aims as similar to
those of Euripides. Indeed he grumbles because the
vulgarity of popular taste will not permit him to use

those devices of chorus and messenger, "the sententious chorus and the passionate and weighty nuntius" which gave dignity to Greek tragic art. He goes on to defend himself for producing so little on the ground that, like all authors who write for posterity and not merely to score a temporary success, he has to work very slowly and very carefully. It is always unwise to disregard what an author tells us about his own work, however surprising it may seem at first hearing. It is unwise with Webster. For, as a matter of fact, a more considered study of his work reveals that it was, in truth, consistent with his aims. With Shakespeare he stands apart from the other Elizabethans as an author who, while accepting the dramatic conventions of his time, turns them to a different and higher purpose.

Not in the same way as Shakespeare; and not so obviously. Shakespeare elevated melodrama by humanising it. He made his characters so like real people that the preposterous stories in which they take part became both convincing and poignant to us. He also makes use of the freedom allowed by the Elizabethan theatre, its mixture of farce and horror and romance, to give an impression of the heterogeneous diversity of real life. Webster could not do these things; he had neither Shakespeare's sense of character nor his breadth of sympathy. Where he rose above his contemporaries was in intellectual and spiritual insight. He uses the Elizabethan freedom to express a vision of the conflict of spiritual forces that, in his view, lie behind the appearances of life as we see it. This is what gives his work unity and significance.

His vision is a moral one. Webster sees life as a struggle between right and wrong. Or rather between good and evil. Here we come to one of the key facts about him. He was a child of his age; the age of the Reformation: and he conceived morality in religious terms. An act to him was wrong, not because it interfered with the happiness of man in this world, but because it was a sin; a breach of the eternal laws established by the God who created man. Moreover it was a voluntary breach. Here again he reveals himself the child of a Christian society. Men to him are not the helpless sport of an indifferent fate as they were to the Greeks. Possessed of free will, his villains sin deliberately. These evil voluntary acts are the cause of human tragedy. Indeed his subject matter may be summed up as a study of the working of sin in the world. Each play presents us with a picture of an act of sin and its consequences.

A very sombre picture too! Webster seems to agree with the view of life expressed in the dirge sung over his victim by the murderer of the Duchess of Malfi.

> "Of what is it fools make such vain keeping?
> Sin their conception, their birth weeping,
> Their real life a general mist of error,
> Their death a hideous storm of terror."

Webster envisages evil in its most extreme form: and he presents it—so far as this life is concerned—as far more powerful than good. His theology is Calvinistic. The world as seen by him is, of its nature incurably corrupt. To be involved in it is to be inescapably involved in evil: all its apparent beauties are a snare and a delusion. There is a couplet of his, expressing what to him must have been a very important truth: for it occurs in both his plays,

"Glories like glow-worms from far off shine bright,
But looked at near have neither heat nor light."

Ambition, pleasure, beauty, passion, the lust of the
eyes and the pride of life—to look to these for happiness
is to be certain of disappointment and disillusionment.
In monarchical seventeenth century England, the Court
was the chief home of these specious mortal splendours.
Webster makes it his symbol for them. Again and
again, and with passion, he makes his characters warn
mankind against the lure of the Court. "Let my son fly
the courts of princes" cries the virtuous Antonio with
his last breath. And the sinner Vittoria echoes him,

"Oh blessed are they that never saw the Court
And never knew great men but by report."

Nor are the glories of this world merely a source of
disillusionment: they are also dangerous to the soul.
They seduce, they corrupt; to obtain them, man is led
into sin. That breach of the Divine Law which for
Webster is the cause of tragedy comes always from too
violent a desire to win this world's prizes. The wicked
commit their crimes because their treasure is not laid
up in heaven, because their hearts are set on those
glories of our blood and state, which are shadows, not
substantial things.

Webster's melancholy view of life is reflected in the
order he imposes upon human nature. His characters
are ranged in moral divisions; there are the good and
there are the bad. But, since to act strongly one must
believe in the value of worldly activities, only the bad
are active and dynamic. They are of two types. The

first—Vittoria, Brachiano, Ferdinand, the Cardinal—
are the creatures of some ruling passion; lust or ambition
or avarice or hatred. Possessed by an insatiate desire
to satisfy it, they break every law, shut their eyes to
every scruple. The second group is actuated less by
passion, than by cynicism. Flamineo and Bosola are
not blinded by the violence of their desires. On the
contrary they are cold and calculating. But they have a
Machiavellian disbelief in human virtue. Mankind to
them is made up of fools and knaves all equally
struggling for their own ends. The only solid goods are
material wealth and success: and, deliberately rejecting
every moral consideration, they set to work to get them.
Opposed to these two types of villain, stand the good
characters; Isabella, Marcello, Cornelia, Antonio, the
Duchess, noble, pitiful and courageous. In contrast
to the bad, however, they are passive: they cannot
identify themselves with the activities of the sin-tainted
world. Once she has married Antonio, the Duchess
initiates no action. The other good characters never do
anything at all. Helpless victims, they are swept into
the turmoil set up by the furious energy of the wicked.
In the end, more often than not, they are destroyed by
them.

A pessimistic view? Not exactly: in a sense Webster
does believe in the ultimate victory of virtue. The good
are only defeated on the material plane. Morally they
triumph. No amount of suffering corrupts them or
breaks their courage: on the contrary, their virtue
shines even brighter for the blood-stained darkness that
gathers about them. Furthermore, though they may
be destroyed, so also—and far more dreadfully—are
their enemies. God is not mocked, the evil-doer is

caught in the net he has woven for others. And he realises why. It is in the stress that he lays on this realisation that the religious foundation of Webster's view of life strikingly appears. His wickedest characters are never moral idiots, who do not understand the enormity of their own crimes. They may profess to disbelieve in virtue and pour contempt on scruple; but it is against the instinctive promptings of their natures. Before they die they are always forced to recognise the supremacy of that Divine Law, against which they have offended. Even Flamineo, the most hardened of the lot, has within him a sense of the difference between good and evil. But from the cradle he has chosen evil, has ranged himself on the side of the devil. Marcello says of him to their mother,

> "I have heard you say in giving my brother suck
> He took the crucifix between his hands
> And broke a limb off."

Neither his amoralism nor his crimes succeed in wholly silencing the voice of his conscience. As he admits, with a sort of angry impatience,

> "I have lived
> Riotously ill, like some that live in Court,
> And sometimes when my face was full of smiles
> Have felt the maze of conscience in my breast."

As the play rises to its climax, this voice grows louder till, "My life was a black charnel", he cries with his dying breath. His gorgeous and baleful sister also, at the point of death, recognises the operation of Divine justice.

> "Oh, my greatest sin lay in my blood;
> Now my blood pays for it."

And earlier we find her recoiling with genuine horror from Flamineo's suggestion of suicide.

> "Are you grown Atheist? Will you turn your body
> Which is the goodly palace of the soul
> To the soul's slaughterhouse . . .
> I prithee yet remember
> Millions are now in graves, which at the last day
> Like mandrakes shall rise shrieking."

The villains in *The Duchess of Malfi* are not less aware of their own sinfulness. The pangs of outraged conscience drive the Cardinal to despair and send Ferdinand raving mad; Bosola's sense of guilt leads him at the last to repent. Always at the end of Webster's plays the Divine Law is vindicated. The final scene of each presents a new and virtuous generation entering to re-establish that moral order which has been destroyed by the acts of sin which have caused the tragedy.

And such then is Webster's tragic vision of the world: a fallen place in which suffering outweighs happiness and all activities are tainted with sin; where evil is the controlling force, and good—just because it is good—is inevitably quietest; hoping, at best and with luck, to slip through the tempest of existence, unnoticed. Yet it is also a place where the moral law cannot be thwarted indefinitely. So that finally evil destroys itself, justice is vindicated.

> "Let guilty men remember their back deeds
> Do lean on crutches made of slender reeds."

In this, the final couplet of *The White Devil*, Webster states the moral truth which the whole preceding drama has been designed to illustrate. The last lines of *The Duchess of Malfi* propound the converse truth:

"Integrity of life is fame's best friend, 1167746
Which nobly, beyond death, shall crown the end."

Heaven is just, for all the apparent horror of man's life. In the end virtue is glorified; but only beyond death.

Let us examine how this view of life exhibits itself in the action of each play. The key figure therefore is always a villain; one of Webster's deliberate intellectual sinners. For since Webster was primarily a man of intellect concerned with ideas, it is the intellectual sinner who interests him most. What happens to a man who directs his life, consciously and calculatedly in defiance of the Divine Law? This is the question that absorbs Webster. He studies it in two diverse examples. In *The White Devil* the deliberate sinner is Flamineo. He is the typical Machiavellian Italian adventurer, as he appeared to an English Protestant eye, ruthless, cynical, consciously anti-moral, living only to advance his fortunes. He sees the best chance of doing this, by making use of the adulterous passion which the Duke Brachiano has conceived for his beautiful sister. He plots to bring them together, and is led by his plots to commit one crime after another, each worse than the last. First he instigates their adultery, then he arranges the murder of Brachiano's wife and Vittoria's husband. Horror at his crimes provokes the wrath of Marcello, his virtuous brother; he kills Marcello in a rage; Cornelia their mother goes mad with grief. Flamineo is thus responsible for his mother's madness as well as his brother's murder. Up to this point his schemes have been successful. Now, however, Divine justice begins to operate to bring punishment on to the sinner. Brachiano is killed in revenge for his wife's death. It looks as if a similar vengeance will soon fall upon Vittoria and Flamineo. Flamineo realises this, he is filled with gloomy apprehensions as to his future; and these are further darkened by spiritual terrors. With the decline of his fortune a profound melancholy, shot through with agonising shafts of guilty fear, fills his breast; incarnating itself in superstitious premonitions of misfortune, and shuddering conjectures as to the ultimate fate of his soul. Brachiano's ghost appears before him:

"What a mockery hath death made thee! (cries
    Flamineo) thou look'st sad.
In what place art thou? In yon starry gallery?
Or in the cursed dungeon?—No? not speak?
Pray, sir, resolve me, what religion's best
For a man to die in? or is it in your knowledge
To answer me how long I have to live?"

Desperately he tries to put his fears by; and concentrates on devising some scheme to save him from his enemies. In order to discover whether he can trust his sister to stand by him, he concocts a fantastic hoax, which involves her agreeing to kill herself with him in a suicide pact. It reveals that he cannot trust her; she is ready to kill him but not herself. The evil-doer has no friends, even among his fellow criminals. What right has he to expect loyalty, when his own actions are founded on a considered repudiation of all but self-interested motives? At this point the avengers arrive to kill him. His last speeches disclose Flamineo's final state of mind. He is not repentant. By now he has become a damned soul, and, as such, incapable of repentance. To the last he speaks with a defiant mocking courage. But it masks an absolute despair. Though no longer capable of appreciating the value of good, he yet realises that evil-doing is also profitless. Like Macbeth, Shakespeare's parallel study of a soul's damnation, he has come to think that life is a tale told by an idiot, signifying nothing, and falls back on a complete nihilism.

"I do not look
Who went before nor who shall follow me;
No, at myself I will begin and end . . .
This busy trade of life appears most vain,
Since rest breeds rest where all seek pain by pain."

In *The Duchess of Malfi* the development is different. For here the intellectual villain Bosola is not wholly given up to the devil. There is a strain of good in him; and in the end this strain of good leads him not to damnation but to repentance. From the first his amorality is shown to be the result largely of harsh circumstances, and as such more excusable. He is a middle-aged soldier of fortune, so embittered by poverty, ingratitude and bad luck, that he is ready to yield to any temptation that comes his way. Why be scrupulous in a wholly unscrupulous world? Ferdinand and the Cardinal take advantage of his desperate mood and make him their creature in their plots against their sister, the Duchess. Under their pressure, he proceeds, like Flamineo, from crime to crime. First he spies on the Duchess, who trusts him; then he betrays her secret; then when the brothers begin to wreak vengeance on her, he becomes first her torturer, afterwards her murderer. But he has never liked his task from the beginning. As it gets more odious, he recoils more and more, receives the brothers' orders with a kind of bitter detachment, praises her courage to them, talks to her, even while he is engineering her torments, with a strange melancholy irony. Finally in the magnificent scene when he stands with the Duke Ferdinand by her dead body, he finds himself unable any longer to shut his ears to the clamour of conscience. The spectacle of his victim, dead, innocent and beautiful, brings home to him the full horror of what he has done:

> "I stand like one
> That long hath taken a sweet and golden dream:
> I am angry with myself now that I wake . . .
> I would not change my peace of conscience
> For all the wealth of Europe."

In the last section of the play he tries to make amends for his sins, seeks out Antonio, the Duchess' husband, to tell him the truth and offer him assistance in bringing justice on her brothers. But only with partial success; the brothers are killed, it is true, but so is Antonio. And, by a wonderful stroke of dramatic irony, he falls by Bosola's hand: in the darkness Bosola has mistaken him for the Cardinal. For, so Webster seems to say, the moral law is inexorable. We cannot undo the evil we have committed. Indeed God may punish us by making our efforts the unwitting cause of further evil.

This last section of *The Duchess of Malfi*, it may be noted in passing, illustrates how little Webster has been properly understood even by his admirers. Because the play is called *The Duchess of Malfi*, she has been looked on as its key figure; and her creator has been censured for continuing the play for another act after her death. But though she is the heroine in the sense that she is the chief object of our sympathies, she does not provide the chief motive force in the action; nor is it, in her relation to that action, that the theme of the play is to be found. This theme, as always with Webster, is the act of sin and its consequences. Till these consequences are followed out to their final conclusion, the dramatist's intention is not made plain. Moreover the central figure, as far as that action is concerned, is the man who murders her; the man who has elected, against the promptings of his better self, to be the devil's agent in the drama.

Webster, then, was not so wrong about himself as might at first sight be supposed. So far from being a mere flamboyant sensation-monger, an unthinking composer of eloquent melodramas, he is a stern moral teacher whose plays are carefully designed to enforce the philosophy of human conduct in which he believes. This in itself, however, does not prove the popular view wrong. A hostile critic might say that whatever Webster's intention, the impression they make is all the same, extravagant, irrational and melodramatic, crammed with irrelevancies and horrors that offend alike against taste and probability. The fact that his

D

aims are so serious, make these faults more flagrant
good Grand Guignol is bad tragedy. Once again such
a criticism shows a failure to grasp the nature of
Webster's art. To incarnate his spiritual drama with
the full intensity which it demands he must use symbols:
the battle of heaven and hell cannot be convincingly
conveyed in a mode of humdrum everyday realism.
And Webster's interpretation of this spiritual battle
can only appropriately be expressed in the most
extravagant symbols. The wild and bloody conventions
of Elizabethan melodrama provided a most appropriate
vehicle for conveying his hell-haunted vision of human
existence. Perhaps Ludovico and Duke Ferdinand do
lack rational motive for their terrific crimes. But in
Webster's view people commit crimes, not from rational
motives, but because they are corrupted by that original
sin with which all mortal flesh is tainted, because they
succumb to the promptings of that devil who is always
whispering in human ears suggestions to obey his
diabolical will. We, who live in an unreligious society,
are always asking that the actions of a criminal should
be accounted for to us by some rational and human
cause; poverty, bad upbringing, psychological mal-
adjustment. The Elizabethans, members of society
soaked in the Christian tradition, took for granted that
the soul of every human being is continually the battle-
ground between the forces of spiritual evil and spiritual
good. Superficially a man may commit a sin for a
practical motive; but the practical motive is merely the
means by which the devil has persuaded him to yield
to that inherent inclination to evil implanted in him
from birth. The Elizabethans could believe in
Ferdinand and Iago and Goneril and the rest of them

without having to be told exactly why they were wicked:
everyone has the disposition to be wicked if he chooses
to give in to it.

Again Webster's horrors—his ghosts and torturers—
are not, as with his lesser contemporaries, mere
theatrical devices to awake a pleasing shudder. They
are symbolic incarnations of that spiritual terror and
diabolical delight in suffering, which are, to him,
central features of the human drama. Duke Ferdinand
and the Cardinal are creatures of hell: the prison in
which they confine the Duchess, made hideous by the
clamour of lunatics and the ghastly images of murdered
children, exhibit to us, in visible form, the hell on
earth, which it is their nature to create. Even Webster's
irrelevant scenes of pageantry, little though they have
to do with the plot, contribute essential features to his
picture of human life. Here, moving before us, are
those ceremonies of worldly dignity, of whose superficial
seductive splendour Webster is acutely aware, and whose
fundamental hollowness he is concerned to expose.

Further, the fact that Webster does not write in a
realistic convention allows his imagination full play:
and thus enables him to make sermons into works of
art. Realistically treated, the stories of *The White Devil*
and *The Duchess of Malfi* would be merely painful and
repulsive. But strangely enough in Webster's hands
they become beautiful; they are alight with a dark
gleaming Rembrandt-like splendour. For every episode,
every thought in them comes to us irradiated by the
unearthly leaping flame of their author's creative
vision. Consider the scene in which Vittoria, lying in
Brachiano's arms, suggests to him that he should
murder his wife and her husband:

VITTORIA. To pass away the time, I'll tell your
    grace
A dream I had last night.
    BRACHIANO. Most wishedly.
    VITTORIA. A foolish idle dream.
Methought I walk'd about the mid of night
Into a church-yard where a goodly yew-tree
Spread her large root in ground. Under that yew,
As I sate sadly leaning on a grave
Chequer'd with cross sticks, there came stealing in
Your duchess and my husband: one of them
A pick-axe bore, the other a rusty spade;
And in rough terms they gan to challenge me
About this yew.
    BRACHIANO. That tree?
    VITTORIA. This harmless yew:
They told me my intent was to root up
That well-grown yew, and plant i' the stead of it
A wither'd blackthorn; and for that they vow'd
To bury me alive. My husband straight
With pick-axe gan to dig, and your fell duchess
With shovel, like a Fury, voided out
The earth, and scatter'd bones. Lord, how, methought,
I trembled! and yet, for all this terror,
I could not pray. . . .
When to my rescue there arose, methought,
A whirlwind, which let fall a massy arm
From that strong plant;
And both were struck dead by that sacred yew,
In that base shallow grave that was their due.
    FERDINAND. Excellent devil! she hath taught him in
    a dream
To make away his duchess and her husband.

In real life, even in Elizabethan real life, people do
not instigate murders by relating weird dreams. But
Webster, by conceiving his scene thus, turns an ugly
episode of lust and treachery and assassination into a
thing of sinister magnificence. The strange precise
images set the fancy mysteriously and sublimely astir:
the ear thrills to the subtle muted music of the
versification.

Yet though he beautifies the horror of his scene,
Webster does not soften it. It is here that the fact he
was an Elizabethan was so lucky for him. The
Elizabethan poetic imagination did not shrink from
the grotesque and the horrible. On the contrary,
fantastic and full-blooded, it craved such food and
grew strong on it. Vittoria's dream clothes her evil
suggestion with imaginative splendour; it also brings
out much more clearly than a realistic treatment would
do, the true nature of the act she is promoting; its
spiritual wickedness, its relation to the supernatural
forces of sin and death, of which it is the offspring.
Less ugly than a realist's version of the same incident,
Webster's is also far more penetrating.

Indeed, Webster is a true tragic poet: one who,
facing the most dreadful and baffling facts of human
experience in all their unmitigated horror, yet trans-
mutes them by the depth and grandeur of his vision
into a thing of glory. This is the rarest sort of poet—
and the greatest. Certainly Webster deserves his
growing fame.

THOMAS GRAY

THE POETRY OF THOMAS GRAY

G RAY is one of the authors who have been more read than written about. There are reasons for this. Appreciation of an author, if it is to be profitable, involves more than just making a list of his excellences, taking the reader on a personally-conducted tour, as it were, of his subject's works, stopping to point out outstanding beauties. The critic should interpret as well as exhibit, perceive the relation between particular works in such a way as to discover the general character of the personality that produced them, and to analyse the special compound of talent and temperament which gives his writing its individuality. With Gray, this is hard. For one thing, his work is so diverse that it is not easy to see it as the expression of a single personality. It is odd that this should be so; for he wrote very little. There are not more than a dozen or so of his memorable poems. But among this dozen we find light verse and serious verse, reflective and dramatic, a sonnet on the death of a friend, and an ode composed to celebrate the installation of a Chancellor of Cambridge University. Further, Gray's poems are composed in a highly conventionalised form which obscures the direct revelation of their author's personality. His figure is separated from us by a veil of literary good manners which blurs its edges and subdues its colour.

All the same, personality and figure are there all

right, if we train our eyes to look carefully. The good manners are Gray's special brand of good manners; whether he is being light or serious, personal or public, Gray shows himself as much an individual as Blake or Byron. What, then, is his individuality? As might be expected from the diversity of its expression, it is complex, combining unexpected elements. The first that strikes the critic is the academic. Gray is an outstanding example of the professional man of learning who happened by a chance gift of fortune to be also a poetic artist. No one has ever lived a more intensely academic life. His home background had nothing to offer him, he was a fastidious, scholarly type, incongruously born into the Hogarthian world of commercial London. At nine years old, however, he was sent to Eton: from Eton he proceeded to Cambridge: and at Cambridge—save for a two years' tour of the Continent at the age of twenty-four—he remained for the rest of his life. He never married, and never engaged in any work outside the University. For thirty years his life was divided between scholarship and scholarly pleasures; reading in his rooms at Cambridge, going up to London for a concert or, once a year, taking a stately little holiday in some picturesque part of England, where he fastidiously contemplated medieval ruins and sunset lakes. As much as Walter Pater he represents that peculiar product of the ancient English universities, the scholar-aesthete.

The name Pater, however, suggests a difference. Gray, unlike Pater, lived in the eighteenth century; so he was an eighteenth-century scholar-aesthete. Now this was something very unlike the nineteenth-century type of which Pater is an example. Nineteenth-century aesthetes were spiritual hermits; they fled from the normal world in horror; its interests and its values alike repelled them as barbarous and philistine. Not so their eighteenth-century forebears. For England, in the eighteenth century, was an integrated society in which people agreed to respect each other's interests and united to accept similar standards of value. Often they differed in taste: some liked the town, others liked the country; some were interested in politics, some in hunting, some in learning. But the student did not despise the soldier; the master of foxhounds was proud to quote such Latin tags as he could remember; and the aesthete was not in the least disposed to scorn the avocations of normal active life, or to dismiss its standards as valueless. Certainly Gray was not. Personally, he preferred a life of retirement; but he could admire those who did not; he had, in fact, a certain amount in common with them. Was he not a strong Whig, a full-blooded patriot—he could hardly keep his temper when he thought of the contemptible French—a solid, though broadminded, member of the Church of England, and a believer in the social graces? Donnish provinciality and awkwardness repelled him: and he showed no taste for artistic unconventionality. The people who attracted him were well-bred, well-mannered, and well-dressed. They were also entertaining. For Gray—and this was another difference between him and the Paterian aesthete—had a great deal of humour. His enthusiasm for beauty and romance was always kept rational by the smiling and satirical good sense of his age. Here we come to the second important element in his composition. In addition to being a representative scholar-artist, he was a representative man of the eighteenth-century world.

We have not done with him, though, when we have discovered his typical qualities. Remarkable people are always more than types; they would not be remarkable if they were not. Gray's personality owes its unmistakable flavour to the peculiar bias of his taste, to the peculiar colouring of his temperament. His taste was the expression of his mental life. This, we have seen, was aesthetic: Gray enjoyed things in so far as they appealed to his sense of beauty. "Beauty" is such a misused, shop-soiled word by now that perhaps I may be allowed to stop for a minute and define in what sense I am using it. It is the ordinary, obvious sense we mean when we say: "What a beautiful sunset!" "What a beautiful church!" "What a beautiful piece of music!" We intend to convey by these exclamations that the object in question appeals to our senses, and, through them, to our imagination. A well-cooked mutton-chop appeals to our senses but not, I fancy, to our imagination; so, however agreeable to the palate, it cannot legitimately be called beautiful. An heroic action appeals to our imagination but not to our senses. It can only be called beautiful metaphorically. When I say that Gray found his chief satisfaction in life in what appealed to his sense of beauty, I do not mean mutton-chops or heroic actions, I mean sunsets and churches and music. As a matter of fact, he did like all these things. His sensibility was extremely varied. And such other subjects as appealed to him were in some way associated in his mind with aesthetic pleasure. His interest in botany, for instance, came primarily from the fact that he thought plants beautiful. All the

same, there was another side to him, only second in
importance to his aesthetic sense, namely, his intense
feeling for history. The fact that he had spent his life
amid the ancient groves and mouldering traceried
architecture of Eton and Cambridge, and that his whole
education was steeped in the spirit of historic Greece
and Rome, made him acutely responsive to the
imaginative appeal of past ages.

Such a responsiveness is often regarded as a phenomenon of the Romantic Movement. This has led some
people to say that Gray, just because he liked reading
Norse sagas and looking at fourteenth-century abbeys,
was a romantic before his time. This is all nonsense.
It is true that the sense of the past only achieved
its full development in the time of the Romantics. Not
till Scott wrote the Waverley novels did it show itself
capable of stimulating by its own unaided power a new
and major form of literature. But it was born earlier.
It was the creature of the eighteenth century. Before
then people do not seem to have felt it. Shakespeare
draws medieval barons and Roman senators alike, as
Elizabethan gentlemen; but Pope in his *Eloisa* already
shows signs that he feels nunneries and ruins to be
romantic. By Gray's time a whole group of persons
had grown up who delighted in nothing so much as
letting their imaginations luxuriate in dwelling on
some past period, in noting the quaintness of its
costumes and architecture, and in enjoying the
picturesque charm of its archaic tongue. Plays, for
the first time, were acted by their producers in what
they imagined to be the correct dress of the period
in which they were set: authors composed historical
novels and mock medieval ballads: scholars edited

ancient texts, Horace Walpole built Strawberry Hill.

Why the sense of the past came to birth in the eighteenth century is not certainly known. But I would suggest that the sober rationalism which permeated the general outlook of the age led its more poetic spirits to find contemporary life intolerably prosaic. Their imagination felt constricted by the spectacle of the world of their own time. They therefore sought relief by escaping mentally to the contemplation of other and less rational periods. Since there was no mystery and magic about the coffee-houses and classical architecture of 1750, they looked for them amid the ruins and rusting armour of the age of faith.

Academic persons confined to the humdrum security of college life were peculiarly susceptible to this. And no one more intensely and more sensitively than Gray. Perpendicular architecture, Elizabethan mansions, medieval illuminated manuscripts alike stirred him to dream and to delight. What wild, mysterious visions arose before his mental eye as he listened to the blind Welsh harpist, Barry, singing the traditional folk-songs of his country! How fascinating it was to walk round the panelled chambers of a Tudor manor-house, tracing the patterns on the blackened carving, noting the picturesque details of dress in the portraits that stared down so uncompromisingly from the walls! In his comic poem, *The Long Story*, he lets his mind play in whimsical fantasy on this taste of his.

> In Britaines isle, no matter where,
> An ancient pile of building stands:
> The Huntingdons and Hattons there
> Employed the power of Fairy hands

To raise the ceiling's fretted height,
Each pannel in achievements cloathing,
Rich windows, that exclude the light,
And passages, that lead to nothing.

Full oft within the spatious walls,
When he had fifty winters o'er him,
My grave Lord-Keeper led the brawls;
The seal, and maces, danc'd before him.

His bushy beard, and shoe-strings green,
His high-crown'd hat, and sattin-doublet,
Mov'd the stout heart of England's queen,
Tho' Pope and Spaniard could not trouble it.

When Gray looked at a landscape, immediately,
instinctively he peopled it in imagination with the
figures of those who had lived there in times past.
Here he is writing a letter describing his fancies during
a visit to the ruins of Netley Abbey.

"In the bosom of the woods (concealed from profane
eyes) lie hid the ruins of Netley Abbey; there may be
richer and greater houses of religion, but the Abbot
is content with his situation. See there, at the top
of that hanging meadow, under the shade of those old
trees that bend into a half circle about it, he is walking
slowly (good man!) and bidding his beads for the souls
of his benefactors, interred in that venerable pile
that lies beneath him. Beyond it (the meadow still
descending) nods a thicket of oaks that mask the building, and have excluded a view too garish and luxuriant
for a holy eye; only on either hand they leave an
opening to the blue glittering sea. Did you not observe

how, as that white sail shot by and was lost, he turned and crossed himself to drive the tempter from him that had thrown that distraction in his way? I should tell you that the ferryman who rowed me, a lusty young fellow, told me that he would not for all the world pass a night at the Abbey, (there were such things near it,) though there was a power of money hid there."

Do you notice in this passage how Gray's aesthetic response to the beauty of the scene mingles inextricably with his response to its historic appeal? His aesthetic emotion was always most intense when it was reinforced by his historic interest, when what was beautiful was also evocative of some vanished age.

Indeed, he always tends to see the contemporary world in relation to its historic past. The Eton College of his Ode lies in the shadow of Windsor's ancestral battlements; the school itself is the place where learning "still adores her Henry's holy Shade". Even when he was meditating on the rustic graves in a country churchyard, historic references intrude themselves; village-Hampdens and Miltons, he fancies, may lie buried there: he contrasts the simple funerals of the poor with the pompous obsequies of great persons in some majestic Gothic cathedral,

> Where thro' the long-drawn aisle and fretted vault
> The pealing anthem swells the note of praise.

His attitude to literature itself is largely an historian's attitude. Both in *The Bard* and in *The Progress of Poesy* he directs our mental eye to observe the great poets of the past as they file by, one by one, down the endless corridor of the ages; he sees the development of the art of letters as an historic process. Gray is the first great English writer for whom the imaginative sense of history is an important source of inspiration, the first who consciously cultivates the sense of period.

This inevitably gives an individual colour to his otherwise normal eighteenth-century vision. It is made still more individual by the particular mood in which he surveyed the drama of human existence. This, for all his humour, was predominantly a minor key mood. The circumstances of his early life, an uncongenial home background, and an unhappy family life still further darkened by the shadow of poverty, had made him early aware of the gloomier side of human existence; with the result that his confidence in living was, from the outset of his career, irrevocably damaged. This was why he took up academic life. Shrinking from contact with the rough world, he sought shelter in monastic and solitary seclusion. He found too little stimulus in it to invigorate his vitality. Year after year he idled away his time in aimless study and abortive literary projects—a prey to hypochondria and ennui. True, he had friends whom he loved passionately. But friendship, though it brought him some ecstatic moments, also brought him sorrowful ones. The friendships of the solitary seldom are productive of happiness. If cool, they are not delightful enough to conquer melancholy; if ardent, they are inevitably frustrated of satisfying fulfilment. For they are not founded on a sufficiently stable basis. The friend is liable to drift away to marriage or active life. Conscious of this insecurity the solitary grows suspicious and

E

difficult. Gray was a touchy, uneasy friend, and his intensest friendships generally came to grief. Such experiences did not tend to brighten his spirits. His considered view of life was melancholy: the world was a dangerous place where sorrow is certain and happiness transient. Once more, however, his temperamental outlook was qualified by the age in which he lived. The eighteenth-century point of view was incompatible with that open out-and-out pessimism to which a romantic like Housman could full-bloodedly surrender himself. For one thing, it believed in the golden mean, and disapproved of extremes of any kind. Even if human life was not perfect, it had its good sides: a rational person strove to keep this in mind. Moreover, whatever unpleasantness life on this planet might entail, it had to be lived: and the wise man made the best of it. To give oneself up to lamentation only made things worse.

Nor was it right. The eighteenth century was profoundly moral. The first duty of man, it held, was to pursue virtue; and there was no doubt that suffering, if taken in the right way, was an aid to virtue. Man could learn through it to bear his own sorrows with courage, and to look with sympathy on those of others. Gray's strong religious convictions made him peculiarly conscious of these obligations, with the result that his melancholy was softened, alike by his faith and his good sense. For the most part it was, as he says, a "white melancholy" which,

"though it seldom laughs or dances nor ever amounts to what one calls Joy or Pleasure, yet is a good easy sort of a state. . . . There is another sort, black indeed, which I have now and then felt that has somewhat in it like Tertullian's rule of faith, *credo quia impossibile est*; for it believes, nay is sure, of everything that is unlikely, so it be but frightful; and, on the other hand, excludes and shuts its eyes to the most possible hopes, and everything that is pleasurable; from this the Lord deliver us! for none but he and sunshiny weather can do it."

Such, then, was Gray—a typical eighteenth-century scholar-artist with a peculiarly intense response to the imaginative appeal of the past and whose pervading temper was a sober melancholy. His memorable poems—for some are mere craftsman's exercises— are the characteristic expression of such a man. They divide themselves into two or three categories, in accordance with the different aspects of his complex nature. His three long odes are inspired by the historical and aesthetic strain in him. That on the Installation of the Duke of Grafton as Chancellor of Cambridge was, it is true, originally designed as an occasional piece. But in it Gray takes advantage of the occasion to show us in what particular way Cambridge did appeal to his own imagination. As might be expected, this is historical. For him the groves and courts of the University are haunted by the ghosts of its founders, Margaret of Anjou, Edward III, Henry VI, and Henry VIII; and of the great spirits, Milton and Newton, who had studied there. *The Bard* gives Gray's historical imagination greater scope. The last of the Druids prophesies to Edward I the misfortunes that are to overtake his line: in a sort of murky magnificence, names and events heavy with romantic and historic associations pass in pageant before us. *The Progress of*

Poesy is less historical, more aesthetic. Though in the second part Gray traces the development of poetic art from Greece to Rome and from Rome to England, this historical motive is made subsidiary to an exposition of what the author considers to be the place of poetry in human life. Like Keats's *Ode on a Grecian Urn*, the *Progress of Poesy* is a meditation about the fundamental significance of art. Not at all the same sort of meditation though. The difference between the Augustan and Romantic attitude to life could not appear more vividly than in the difference between these two poems. There is nothing transcendental about Gray's view, no vision of art as an expression of ultimate spiritual reality, where Truth is the same as Beauty and Beauty the same as Truth. Poetry to Gray, as to any other sensible eighteenth-century gentleman, was primarily a pleasure: and the poet so far from being the priest of a mystery was a purveyor of pleasure—"above the great, but", he is careful to point out, "far below the good". But poetry was useful and even educative: a necessary part of the good life, soothing the passions, civilising the heart and manners, celebrating beauty and virtue, and, above all, providing an alleviation to the inevitable ills of the human lot.

The second category of Gray's poems deals with his personal relation to life: his impressions of experience and the conclusions he drew from them. In one poem, indeed—the sonnet on the death of his friend West—he draws no conclusion: the poem is a simple sigh of lamentation. But, in all the other expressions of this phase of his work, sentiment leads to reflection and reflection to a moral. The Eton College Ode shows Gray surveying the scenes of his youth and

observing the unthinking happiness of childhood
through the eyes of a disillusioned maturity. With a
sad irony he draws his conclusion:

Where ignorance is bliss, 'tis folly to be wise.

The *Ode on the Spring* is inspired by the spectacle of a
fine day in early spring, with the buds hastening to
open and the insects busily humming. How like the
activities of the world of men! says Gray, and hardly
more ephemeral. But once more irony steps in—Who
is he to condemn? It is true he has chosen to be
spectator rather than actor: but he is no wiser than
the actors and perhaps enjoys himself less. The
unfinished *Ode on Vicissitude* points yet another moral.
Though life is a chequer-work of good and ill, sad and
happy, we ought not to repine: perhaps without the
sadness we should enjoy the intervals of happiness
less than we do. The Adversity Ode is sterner in tone.
Adversity is a trial sent by God to school us to virtue,
if we are strong enough to profit by it. Finally there is
the *Elegy*. Here the sight of the graveyard stirs the
poet to meditate on the life of man in relation to its
inevitable end. Death, he perceives, dwarfs human
differences. There is not much to choose between the
great and the humble, once they are in the grave. It
may be that there never was; it may be that in the
obscure graveyard lie persons who but for untoward
circumstances would have been as famous as Milton
and Hampden. The thought, however, does not sadden
him; if circumstances prevented them achieving great
fame, circumstances also saved them from committing
great crimes. Yet there is a special pathos in these

obscure tombs; the crude inscriptions on the clumsy monuments are so poignant a reminder of the vain longing of all men, however humble, to be loved and to be remembered. This brings Gray round to himself. How does he expect to be remembered? Not as a happy man: he has been sad, obscure, misunderstood. Yet, he reminds himself with his customary balance, there have been alleviations. He has known friendship, loved learning, and attained, in part at least, to virtue. Soberly, but with faith, he resigns himself to the judgement of his God.

This group of poems is all concerned with the same thing, the relation of a sensitive contemplative spirit to the thronging, mysterious, tragic, transient world into which he finds himself thrown. For all their formality of phrase, they are consistently and intensely personal.

There remains the brief and brilliant category of Gray's satirical and humorous verse—*The Long Story*, *The Ode on a Cat*, *Hymn to Ignorance*, and the *Impromptu on Lord Holland's House*. Now and again in these poems, more particularly in *The Long Story*, Gray the historian shows his hand; while they all display his scholarly sense of finish. Mainly, however, they reveal Gray the man of the world—Gray the admirer of Pope and the friend of Walpole. In the best eighteenth-century manner he uses his taste and his learning to add wit and grace to the amenities of social life. But they are none the less characteristic for that. As much as pindaric or elegy they contribute essential features to our mental portrait of their author.

Gray's mode of expression is as typical of him as is his choice of themes. His style is pre-eminently an academic style, studied, traditional, highly finished. His standard of finish, indeed, was so high as sometimes to be frustrating. He could take years to complete a brief poem. During the process he sent round fragments to his friends for their advice. Like Mr. James Joyce, though not so publicly, Gray was given to issuing his work while "in progress". Sometimes it remained for ever in this unreposeful condition. He never managed to get the *Ode on Vicissitude* finished at all. His choice of forms, too, is a scholar's choice. Sedulously he goes to the best authors for models. He writes the Pindaric Ode—making a more careful attempt than his predecessors had, exactly to follow Pindar—the Horatian Ode, the classical sonnet, and the orthodox elegy, leading up to its final formal epitaph. His diction is a consciously poetic affair; an artificial diction, deliberately created to be an appropriate vehicle for lofty poetry. "The language of the age", he stated as an axiom, "is never the language of poetry." Certainly his own language was not that of his age—or of any other, for that matter. It is an elaborate compound of the language of those authors whom he most admired: Horace and Virgil, Pope and Dryden, above all, Milton—the youthful Milton who wrote *L'Allegro* and *Lycidas*. For Milton, as the greatest English Master of the artificial style, appealed peculiarly to Gray. Sometimes the influence of one of these poets predominates, sometimes of another, according to which Gray thinks is the best in the kind of verse he is attempting. He follows Pope in satire, Dryden in declamation, Milton in elegiac and picturesque passages. It was from Milton, incidentally, he learnt the evocative power of proper names:

Cold is Cadwallo's tongue,
That hush'd the stormy main:
Brave Urien sleeps upon his craggy bed:
Mountains, ye mourn in vain
Modred, whose magic song
Made huge Plinlimmon bow his cloud-top'd head.

Nor does he just imitate other authors. He openly quotes them. The Pindaric Odes especially are whispering galleries, murmurous with echoes of dead poets' voices—Shakespeare's, Spenser's, Cowley's. Sometimes he will lift a whole passage; the image of Jove's eagle in the second stanza of *The Progress of Poesy* is transplanted from Pindar's First Pythian. Sometimes he will adapt a phrase: "ruddy drops that warm my heart" in *The Bard* is a modification of the "ruddy drops that visit my sad heart" in *Julius Caesar*. Once again, Gray curiously reminds us of a modern author. This device of imbedding other people's phrases in his verse anticipates Mr. T. S. Eliot. Gray's purpose, however, is very different. The quoted phrase is not there to point an ironical contrast as with Mr. Eliot; rather it is inserted to stir the reader's imagination by the literary associations which it evokes. Conscious, as Gray is, of poetry developing in historic process, he wishes to enhance the effect of his own lines by setting astir in the mind memories of those great poets of whom he feels himself the heir.

The trouble about such devices is that they limit the scope of the poem's appeal. Gray's pindarics, like Mr. Eliot's *Waste Land*, can be fully appreciated only by highly educated readers. Indeed, Gray's education was not altogether an advantage to him as a writer. At times his poetry is so clogged with learning as to be obscure. *The Bard* and *The Progress of Poesy* are crowded with allusions that need notes to explain them. While we are painstakingly looking at the notes, our emotional response to the poem grows chilly. In his effort to concentrate his allusion into one polished, pregnant phrase, Gray tends to leave out the facts necessary to make it immediately intelligible:

> The bristled Boar in infant-gore
> Wallows beneath the thorny shade.

To Gray fresh from the libraries of Cambridge this may have seemed lucid enough. But how can the common reader be expected to realise straight away that it refers to Richard III's death at the battle of Bosworth? Like some poets of our own time, Gray seems at moments to forget the difference between a poem and a conundrum.

It is another defect of Gray's academic method—and, it may be added, of his academic temperament—that it involved a certain lack of imaginative heat. Scholars are seldom fiery spirits: Gray's poems are, compared with those of Burns let us say, a touch tepid. This tepidness shows itself in his personifications. Gray is very fond of personifications:

> Warm Charity, the gen'ral Friend,
> With Justice to herself severe,
> And Pity, dropping soft the sadly-pleasing tear.

These personifications are clear and sensible enough. Charity—were she a person—might reasonably be expected to be a friendly one; and Pity to shed tears.

But somehow the effect is lifeless. We feel that—having decided to personify these virtues—Gray deliberately, and with the help of his intellect, gets to work to make suitable puppets in which to incarnate them. On the other hand when Keats speaks of

> Joy, whose hand is ever at his lips
> Bidding adieu;

the impression we get is that Joy spontaneously embodied itself in a living figure, which flashed unbidden, and as in a vision, before the poet's mental eye.

Indeed Gray's head is stronger than his fancy or his passions. Always we are aware in his work of the conscious intellect, planning and pruning: seldom does his inspiration take wing to sweep him up into that empyrean where feeling and thought are one. The words clothe the idea beautifully and aptly and in a garment that could only have been devised by a person of the most refined taste and the highest culture. But they clothe it, they do not embody it. For that absolute union of thought and word which is the mark of the very highest poetry of all, we look to Gray in vain. He had not that intensity of inspiration; and, anyway, education had developed his critical spirit too strongly for him to be able completely to let himself go. His poetry, in fact, illustrates perfectly the characteristic limitations of the academic spirit.

But it also reveals, in the highest degree, its characteristic merits. Always it is disciplined by his intellect and refined by his taste. The matter is rational; Gray never talks nonsense; each poem is logically designed, with a beginning, a middle, and an end. Every line and every phrase has its contribution to make to the general effect; so that the whole gives one that particular satisfaction that comes from seeing a problem completely resolved. Even the best lines—and this is a typical beauty of conscious art—are better in their context than when they are lifted from it. Moreover, though Gray fails to achieve the highest triumphs of expression, he maintains a consistently high level of style—better than some greater men do. No doubt it is a style that takes getting used to: artificial styles always do. We must accustom ourselves to the tropes and the antitheses, the abstractions, classical allusions and grandiose periphrases which are his habitual mode of utterance. They are as much a part of it as the garlands and trophies which ornament a piece of baroque architecture; for Gray lived in the baroque period and shared its taste. A poem like *The Progress of Poesy* is like nothing so much as some big decorative painting of the period in which, posed gracefully on an amber-coloured cloud, allegorical figures representing the arts and the passions offer ceremonious homage to the goddesses of Poetry or Beauty:

Slow melting strains their Queen's approach declare:
Where'er she turns the Graces homage pay.
With arms sublime, that float upon the air,
In gliding state she wins her easy way:
O'er her warm cheek, and rising bosom, move
The bloom of young Desire, and purple light of Love.

Does not that recall some radiant, florid ceiling painted by Tiepolo?

And it is executed with a similar virtuosity. Gray attempts the most complex and difficult metres. His work is thickly embroidered with image and epigram. But the images and epigrams are appropriate. Every cadence is both musical in itself and an apt echo of the sense:

> Say, has he giv'n in vain the heav'nly Muse?
> Night, and all her sickly dews,
> Her Spectres wan, and Birds of boding cry,
> He gives to range the dreary sky:
> Till down the eastern cliffs afar
> Hyperion's march they spy, and glittering shafts
>   of war.

Once again, I am quoting from *The Progress of Poesy*: for it is in these Pindaric Odes that Gray's virtuosity appears most conspicuously. They are not, however, his most successful works. For in them he is dealing with subject-matter which does reveal his limitations. This is especially true of *The Bard*. Here Gray tries to write dramatically; he addresses us in the person of a medieval druid about to commit suicide. Such a rôle does not suit him. Gray was excited by reading about druids; but he was not at all like a druid himself. Nor had he the kind of imagination convincingly to impersonate one. He tried very hard—"I felt myself the Bard", he said—but, alas, the result of all his efforts was only a stagey, if stylish, example of eighteenth-century rhetoric, elaborately decked up with the ornaments of a Strawberry Hill Mock-Gothic. In *The Progress of Poesy* Gray wisely refrains from any attempt at impersonation and the result is far more

successful. Indeed, in its way, the poem is a triumph.
But a triumph of style rather than substance. The
pleasure we get from the work is that given by watching
a master-craftsman magnificently displaying his skill
in an exercise on a given conventional theme.

No—Gray writes best when he does not try a lofty
flight of imagination, but, with his feet planted firmly
on the earth, comments lightly or gravely on the world
he himself knew. Here, once more, he is typical of his
period. Eighteenth-century writers are, most of them,
not so much concerned with the inward and spiritual
as with the social and moral aspects of existence—less
with man the solitary soul in relation to the ideal
and the visionary, than with man the social animal in
relation to the people and the age in which he finds
himself. For all he lived a life of retirement, Gray is no
exception to his contemporaries. The region of romance
and art in which he liked to take refuge was to him a
place of pleasant distraction, not the home of a deeper
spiritual life, as it was for Blake, for instance. Even
when in the *Ode on the Spring* he contrasts his own inactive
existence with that of his fellows, his eye is on them;
his interest is to see how his life relates to theirs. And
the thoughts stirred in him by his contemplations here,
as also in his Eton ode, are of the straightforward kind
which they could understand. So might any thoughtful
person feel on a spring day, or when revisiting their
old school. What Johnson said of *The Elegy in a
Country Churchyard* is equally true of Gray's other elegiac
pieces. "They abound with sentiments to which every
bosom returns an echo." Indeed Gray's relative lack
of originality made him peculiarly able to speak for the
common run of mankind. But he spoke for them in

words they could not have found for themselves. Poetry, says Pope, should be "what oft was thought but ne'er so well expressed". This is not true of all poetry. But it is true of Gray's. The fact that he was an exquisite artist made it possible for him to express the commonplace with an eloquence and a nobility that turn it into immortal poetry. Moreover, his vision is deepened and enriched by his historic sense. His meditations in the churchyard acquire a monumental quality, because they seem to refer to it at any time during its immemorial history: his reflections on his Eton schooldays gain universality from the fact that he perceives his own sojourn there as only an episode in the School's life, and his personal emotions about it as the recurrent emotion of generations of Etonians.

These reflective poems, too, are more moving than the Pindaric Odes. No wonder: they were the product of the deepest emotional crisis of his life. The Pindarics were written in his tranquil middle age; these other poems, all except the *Elegy*, in the later months of 1742; and the *Elegy*, completed a few years later, is a final comment on the same phase of his experience. Two events produced this phase. Gray's prospects were very dark; poverty was forcing him back to take up life at Cambridge at a moment when he felt a strong reaction against it: and the pair of friends who were his chief source of happiness were during this time lost to him. He quarrelled with Walpole, and West died. Under the combined stress of these misfortunes his emotional agitation rose to a pitch which found vent in an unprecedented outburst of poetic activity. Even when inspired by such an impulse, the result is not exactly passionate: but it is heartfelt. The sentiment it expresses has its birth in the very foundations of the poet's nature; it is distilled from the experience of a lifetime. Let me quote the sonnet on the death of West:

> In vain to me the smileing Mornings shine,
>   And redning Phœbus lifts his golden Fire:
> The Birds in vain their amorous Descant joyn;
>   Or chearful Fields resume their green Attire:
> These Ears, alas! for other Notes repine,
>   A different Object do these Eyes require.
> My lonely Anguish melts no Heart, but mine;
>   And in my Breast the imperfect Joys expire.
> Yet Morning smiles the busy Race to chear,
>   And new-born Pleasure brings to happier Men:
> The Fields to all their wonted Tribute bear:
>   To warm their little Loves the Birds complain:
> I fruitless mourn to him, that cannot hear,
>   And weep the more because I weep in vain.

Is not this poignant? Once more, you will remark, its effect is intensified by what I can only call Gray's commonplaceness. It is interesting in this connection to compare it with a more famous lamentation over the dead, with *Lycidas*. Poetically, of course, it is of a lower order. Gray had nothing like Milton's imaginative and verbal genius. All the same, and just because Gray was not so original a genius, his poem does something that Milton's does not. It expresses exactly what the average person does feel when someone he loves dies.

Nor does its eighteenth-century formality weaken its emotional force. On the contrary, it makes it seem more authentic. Personal feelings of this kind always present peculiar difficulties to a poet; for it is so hard to express them without sentimentality, so hard for the poet not to seem as if he was calculatedly exploiting his private emotions in order to bring tears to the eyes of his readers. The more colloquial and informal the language he uses, the more likely this is to happen. Gray's formality acts as a filter of good-mannered reticence through which his private grief comes to us, purged of any taint of sentimentality or exhibitionism, and with a pathos that seems all the more genuine because it is unemphasized:

> I fruitless mourn to him, that cannot hear,
>   And weep the more because I weep in vain.

In lines like these, as in the more famous *Elegy*, the two dominant strains in Gray serve each to strengthen the effect of the other. The fastidious artist and the eighteenth-century gentleman combine to produce something that is in its way both perfect and profound.

Equally perfect and from similar causes is Gray's lighter verse. Light verse rarely attains classical quality. Either it is so conversational and careless as to be vulgar; or, if the author tries to dignify it by a more stately style, he only succeeds in being pedantically facetious. The writer of light verse walks a narrow path between the abysses of donnish jocularity on the one hand, and music-hall slanginess on the other. Gray's curiously compounded nature enabled him to keep to this path unerringly. He is never pedantic, he jests with the elegant ease of a man of fashion. But the solid foundation of scholarly taste, which underlies everything he writes, gives his most frivolous improvisation distinction. Nor do those characteristics of his

style which sometimes impede our appreciation of his
other work trouble us here. In light verse it does not
matter if we are aware of the intellectual process at
work. It is right in comedy that the head should
rule the heart and fancy. As for Gray's baroque
conventionalities of phrase, these, when introduced,
as it were, with a smile, enhance his wit by a delightful
ironical stylishness:

> The hapless Nymph with wonder saw:
> A whisker first and then a claw,
>   With many an ardent wish,
> She stretch'd in vain to reach the prize.
> What female heart can gold despise?
>   What Cat's averse to fish?

"The Cat", says Dr. Johnson caustically, "is called a
nymph, with some violence both to language and sense".
Perhaps she is. Nevertheless—and one can dare to say
so aloud now Dr. Johnson is no longer with us—the
effect is charming.

Gray has two masterpieces in this lighter vein; these
lines on the Cat, and those on the artificial ruins put
up by Lord Holland at Kingsgate. The poem on the
Cat is the more exquisite; in its own brief way as
enchanting a mixture of wit and prettiness as *The Rape
of the Lock* itself. But the bitter brilliance of the other
shows that, had he chosen, Gray could equally have
rivalled Pope as a satirist in the grand manner:

Old and abandon'd by each venal friend
   Here Holland took the pious resolution
To smuggle some few years and strive to mend
   A broken character and constitution.

F

On this congenial spot he fix'd his choice,
  Earl Godwin trembled for his neighbouring sand,
Here Seagulls scream and cormorants rejoice,
  And Mariners tho' shipwreckt dread to land,
Here reign the blustring north and blighting east,
  No tree is heard to whisper, bird to sing,
Yet nature cannot furnish out the feast,
  Art he invokes new horrors still to bring:
Now mouldring fanes and battlements arise,
  Arches and turrets nodding to their fall,
Unpeopled palaces delude his eyes,
  And mimick desolation covers all.
Ah, said the sighing Peer, had Bute been true
  Nor Shelburn's, Rigby's, Calcraft's friendship vain,
Far other scenes than these had bless'd our view
  And realis'd the ruins that we feign.
Purg'd by the sword and beautifyed by fire,
  Then had we seen proud London's hated walls,
Owls might have hooted in St. Peters Quire,
  And foxes stunk and litter'd in St. Pauls.

Horace Walpole said that "Humour was Gray's natural and original turn, that he never wrote anything easily but things of Humour". In view of these poems, it is hard to disagree with him. Nowhere else does Gray's virtuosity seem so effortless; nowhere else does he write with the same spontaneity and gusto. For once Gray seems to be sailing with the wind behind him the whole way. Of all his work, his light verse appears the most inspired.

How far this means that it is also the most precious is a different problem. A very big one too: it opens the whole question as to whether comic art can of its nature be equal in significance to grave art, whether the humorist's view of things is always comparatively speaking, a superficial view. This takes us into deep waters; too deep to be fathomed in the brief close of an essay like the present. But the issue is, surely, a more doubtful one than those earnest personages, the professional critics of literature, appear for the most part to think.

FANNY BURNEY

FANNY BURNEY

FEW first novels have been more successful than *Evelina*. Not only was it a best-seller, but it won enthusiastic praise from the most distinguished minds of the age. "Worthy of Richardson at his best", said Burke: Dr. Johnson majestically expressed a desire to meet its author. Nor was *Evelina's* success a flash in the pan. *Cecilia*, appearing a few years later, met with, if possible, greater acclamation. And though her third and fourth novels—*Camilla* and *The Wanderer* —were less admired, Fanny Burney's reputation remained very high. In fact, no less a person than Jane Austen thought *Camilla* a masterpiece. To-day, it must be admitted, all this enthusiasm seems exaggerated. Compared with the greatest novels, Fanny Burney's look a trifle thin. All the same it is possible to see why they made such a sensation among contemporaries. For they were something new. In Fanny Burney's hands the novel took a step forward which was to have enormous consequences. Her stories represent the entry of the woman, or perhaps one should say the lady, into English fiction.

The English novel was created—as every history of literature tells us—by Richardson and Fielding. They conceived it on different lines. Richardson was the first dramatic novelist. His subject is the clash of character; and he exhibits it by an elaborate analysis of the processes of heart and conscience in a given situation. Fielding is the first panoramic novelist.

His aim is to give a broad humorous picture of the varieties of the human scene. His plots are merely the framework on which he stretches this picture. Fanny Burney derives from both, but more from Fielding. Here she was like most of her countrymen. Richardson's influence was strongest on the Continent; but the English, the lazy, unintrospective English, with their delight in humour and their suspicion of any entertainment that demanded a strenuous intellectual effort, tended to follow Fielding. Fanny Burney had a typically English talent; she was a bright, light, humorous observer of the outward scene, not a psychological analyst; and, like Fielding, what attracted her about the novel form was the opportunity it provided for giving an entertaining picture of the world about her. In their main lines her novels are of the Fielding type, satirical panoramas of society centring upon an agreeable hero and heroine, and held together rather loosely by a symmetrical plot, culminating in their happy marriage. Perhaps the shortest way to sum up her place in the history of English Letters is to say that she was the first writer to translate the Fielding-type of novel into the feminine key.

This meant altering it considerably. Fielding was an intensely masculine character: Fanny Burney was equally intensely feminine, using the word, it must be owned, not wholly in its best sense. She was an English lady of a recognisable type, lively, civilised, and, within certain limits, extremely observant, but petty, fussy, a slave to convention and far too easily shocked. *Evelina*, we recall, is so horrified at the coarseness of *Love for Love* that she is quite unable to get any pleasure out of its brilliance. This is not at all like

Fielding: and such a difference of outlook imposed a
very different perspective on her creator's panorama of
English society.   Inevitably it is much narrower.
Fielding is free to move his heroes all over the place:
now they are talking to squires, now to gamekeepers,
now they are flirting with ladies of title in London
boudoirs, now drinking at the tavern with the postboy,
now at a ball, now at a gaming-house, now following
the hunt, now in Newgate jail.   Their sisters—Miss
Burney's heroines—were shut off from all these phases
of life except those to be observed at the squire's house,
the boudoir, and the ball.   Even there the scope of her
observation was limited by convention.   She heard only
such parts of the conversation as were thought suitable
for a young lady's ears.   In compensation, however,
she had time to examine in great detail what she was
permitted to see—Fielding's young men never observed
the texture of social intercourse so minutely—and,
under the microscope of her undeviating attention, one
aspect of the social scene stood out as it had never
stood out to him.   This was its social distinctions.
Social distinctions, no doubt, are a feature of the picture
of life presented by Miss Burney's predecessors; for
England in the eighteenth century was—even more
than it is now—a hierarchical society.   Differences of
rank were one of its outstanding characteristics.   But
Fielding and Smollett and the rest of them surveyed
the world with too broad a sweep to note more than
their salient features.   It was different for a woman.
She could only satisfy her adventurousness and curiosity
within the confines of the different social worlds into
which respectable girls were allowed to go.   She could
not visit Newgate, or the tavern, or the gaming-house;

she could only move from country society to town
society, from the fashionable to the dowdy, from the
elegant to the vulgar, from the aristocratic to the
professional classes. The diversity of her panorama was
limited by the diversity she could find included in this
area. It was not a fatal limitation. By nature, women
are observers of those minutiæ of manners in which
the subtler social distinctions reveal themselves. Fanny
Burney seized her opportunity with avidity. In her
hands, for the first time in the English novel, social
distinctions are the dominant subject of the story. She
is the first novelist—though very far from being the
last—to make a thorough study of snobbery.

Further, although her plots are constructed within
the same convention as Fielding's, their emphasis is
different. The Fielding type of plot turns on love and
marriage; but Fielding was not particularly interested
in the feelings of his hero and heroine for each other.
Tom loves Sophia; Sophia loves Tom. From time to
time Sophia learns of some lapse of Tom's which
temporarily puts her off him. But when it is explained,
or apologised for, back her sentiment flows into its
original channel without comment on the part of her
creator. Fielding, like most very masculine men, has
no objective interest in observing the process of courtship. Fanny Burney had; and she gives up a great deal
of her space to tracing it.

It is in her treatment of this aspect of her theme that
she reveals the influence of Richardson. Though she
did not see life as a whole dramatically, one drama
did interest her: the central drama of any young lady's
life—the drama of getting married. Confronted with this
spectacle she becomes for the time being a psychologist.

How does a young lady feel on first meeting a marriageable young man? How does she discover her growing sentiments towards him? What steps does she take to check or to cherish them? How far by observing his behaviour, governed as it is outwardly by the rules of formal good manners, is she able to interpret the fluctuation of his feelings towards her? In Fanny Burney's novels, for the first time, the process of an ordinary, legitimate, everyday courtship becomes the central theme of an English novel.

Richardson was bound to be her master here. He was the master of any English novelist who sought to analyse feeling. In *Sir Charles Grandison* he had used his skill to illuminate the complicated hopes and fears, the scruples of honour and modesty and refinement, which agitated the breast of Miss Harriet Byron at the sight of the awful perfections of Sir Charles. However, Miss Burney is no mere imitator of Richardson. A woman herself, she could enter into a girl's feelings much more realistically than he could. And anyway Richardson's mind tended always to pierce beneath a particular drama, to explore the fundamental moral situation that it illustrates. Besides, with him, analysis of character occupies most of the book. With Fanny Burney the courtship which is the subject of analysis is merely the central theme of the action; and the action is, as we have seen, secondary to her picture of society as a whole.

Fanny Burney's range, then, the area of experience in which her creative talent shows itself, is that concerned with respectable society and respectable courtship. Her three chief books all follow the same plan. An inexperienced young girl—Evelina or Cecilia or

Camilla—is cast into the social world. We see it through her clear innocent eyes in all its variety.* Soon —for Fanny Burney's heroines are usually both lovely and financially eligible—a cloud of suitors surrounds her. By the end of the book she has chosen a husband. In the meantime she has visited London, the country— usually a spa—has moved in good society and bad. By the end, in addition to getting married, she has managed to acquire a knowledge of the world.

It is an excellent subject for a novelist, and in many ways Fanny Burney was well equipped to do it justice. She had a vigorous, varied, vivacious talent that could control and vitalise a great deal of diverse material. Further, she was a natural story-teller: she gets the plot going at once, and sustains it by an unflagging talent for inventing incidents. Even though these are sometimes unconvincing, they do not bore the reader. Always they are related with spirit. And anyway no single one goes on too long. After the long-windedness of many eighteenth-century novels Fanny Burney's comes as a welcome relief. Moreover—it was her outstanding talent—she was extremely observant of the surface of existence. Fanny Burney can bring to life not only her central figures but the whole world they live in. To open *Cecilia* or *Evelina* is to be transported straight into eighteenth-century London, crowded, shrill, diverse, bustling, with its curious blend of elegance and crudeness, of ceremoniousness and brutality. Now we are with the middle classes, gossiping

* The original conception of this theme seems also to have been suggested by *Sir Charles Grandison*, which opens with Harriet Byron's introduction, as an inexperienced young girl, to London society. But Richardson is not interested in the social scene, and does not explore the possibilities for describing it suggested by his scheme.

with a merchant in the room behind his shop, or out for an evening's pleasure with a flashy city beau at the shilling ball at Hampstead; now we are moving in the beau monde at a masquerade, or at Ranelagh rubbing shoulders with languid fops and rattle-pated ladies; now crowding up the stairs to the Italian Opera, now at a fashionable concert overhearing the conversation of two frivolous debutantes:

". . . though there was an excellent concert in which several capital performers played and sung, she found it impossible to hear a note, as she chanced to be sitting just by Miss Leeson, and two other young ladies who were paying one another compliments upon their dress and their looks, settling to dance in the same cotillon, guessing who would begin the minuets, and wondering there were not more gentlemen. Yet in the midst of this unmeaning conversation . . . not one of them failed, from time to time to exclaim with great rapture 'What sweet music!'—'Oh, how charming!'—'Did you ever hear anything so delightful?' "

In each place Fanny Burney picks out infallibly the particular detail of scene or speech that brings it alive and stirring before our mental eye. And she relates what she sees with just that touch of slight caricature, that stroke of Hogarthian style, which gives it aesthetic life and quality.

Nor is her observation confined to the general scene. She had a lively gift for drawing individual character. It shows itself in two ways. Her most typical successes are in that tradition of realistic humorous portraiture which she learnt from Fielding and Smollett, and which

they in their turn had inherited from the comic drama
—"character parts", to use a stage phrase, made up of
one or two strongly marked idiosyncrasies, drawn in a
convention of slight caricature, and revealing themselves directly in dialogue: Evelina's vulgar cousins,
the Branghtons, and their friend Mr. Smith; the
fashionables who aroused the contempt of Cecilia,
Miss Larolles, Miss Leeson, the absurd Mr. Meadows
who thought it dowdy to appear to enjoy anything.
Captain Aresby with his conversation all scattered over
with French phrases, the miserly Mr. Briggs. Fanny
Burney does not present them with subtlety. The
Branghtons are always vulgar, Meadows is always
bored, Miss Larolles is always chattering like a magpie.
All the same, they are not mere conventional types.
Their creator had an extremely sharp ear for dialogue,
for the particular accent of silliness or pomposity
which distinguishes one fool from another. She may
represent these figures only in one aspect, but that aspect
is drawn straight from life; and life still throbs in it.

Listen to the Branghtons persuaded by their genteel
cousin to attend an opera for the first time.

"At the end of the first act, as the green curtain
dropped to prepare for the dance, they imagined that
the opera was done; and Mr. Branghton expressed
great indignation that he had been *tricked* out of his
money with so little trouble. 'Now if any Englishman
was to do such an impudent thing as this,' he said,
'why, he'd be pelted; but here, one of these outlandish
gentry may do just what he pleases, and come on, and
squeak out a song or two, and then pocket your money
without further ceremony'.

"However, so determined he was to be dissatisfied, that, before the conclusion of the third act, he found still more fault with the opera for being too long; and wondered whether they thought their singing good enough to serve us for supper.

"During the symphony of a song of Signor Millico's, in the second act, young Mr. Branghton said, 'It's my belief that that fellow's going to sing another song. Why, there's nothing but singing! I wonder when they'll speak.'

"This song, which was slow and pathetic, caught all my attention, and I lean'd my head forward to avoid hearing their observations, that I might listen without interruption: but, upon turning round, when the song was over, I found that I was the object of general diversion to the whole party; for the Miss Branghtons were tittering, and the two gentlemen making signs and faces at me, implying their contempt of my affectation.

"This discovery determined me to appear as inattentive as themselves; but I was very much provoked at being thus prevented enjoying the only pleasure, which, in such a party, was within my power.

" 'So Miss,' said Mr. Branghton, 'you're quite in the fashion, I see; so you like operas? Well, I'm not so polite; I can't like nonsense, let it be never so much the taste.'

" 'But pray, Miss,' said the son, 'what makes that fellow look so doleful while he is singing?'

" 'Probably because the character he performs is in distress.'

" 'Why, then, I think he might as well let alone singing till he's in better cue: it's out of all nature for a

man to be piping when he's in distress. For my part,
I never sing but when I'm merry; yet I love a song as
well as most people.'

"When the curtain dropped they all rejoiced.

" 'How do *you* like it?'—and 'How do *you* like it?'
passed from one to another with looks of the utmost
contempt. 'As for me,' said Mr. Branghton, 'they've
caught me once; but if ever they do again, I'll give 'em
leave to sing me to Bedlam for my pains: for such a
heap of stuff never did I hear; there isn't one ounce of
sense in the whole Opera, nothing but one continued
squeaking and squalling from beginning to end.'

" 'It I had been in the pit,' said Madame Duval,
'I should have liked it vastly, for music is my passion,
but sitting in such a place as this, is quite unbearable.'

"Miss Branghton, looking at me, declared, that she
was not *genteel* enough to admire it.

"Miss Polly confessed, that, if they would but sing
English she would like it *very well*.

"The brother wished he could raise a riot in the
house, because then he might get his money again.

"And, finally, they all agreed, that it was *monstrous
dear.*"

This is dreadfully convincing; no wonder poor
Evelina felt awkward at being seen with such com-
panions. Indeed, Fanny Burney is never better than
when conveying social embarrassments of this kind.
Evelina, confronted at this very Opera by the dashing
Sir Clement Willoughby; or, on another occasion,
forced by the Branghtons to ask the awe-inspiring
Lord Orville to give her the use of his carriage—in these
scenes embarrassment is portrayed with such vividness

as to render them painful to read about. Perhaps too painful: Evelina could hardly have suffered more had she been caught committing a crime; and, after all, it is not a crime to be found by genteel people in vulgar company. Hard though Fanny Burney was on other snobs, I am afraid she herself cannot be altogether acquitted of snobbishness. A social lapse was to her a tragedy. Still, the emotion she puts into them makes her accounts of such lapses more convincingly realistic. To a shy young girl, taking her first tentative steps on to the stage of the great world, a social lapse has its tragic side.

Fanny Burney's mastery over character is not exclusively confined to these satiric types. At times she shows also an insight that enables her to penetrate beneath the surface of personality.

"And if Mr. Delvile was shunned through hatred, his lady no less was avoided through fear; high spirited and fastidious, she was easily wearied and disgusted, she bore neither frailty nor folly—those two principal ingredients in human nature! She required, to obtain her favour, the union of virtue and abilities with elegance, which meeting but rarely, she was rarely disposed to be pleased; and disdaining to conceal either contempt or aversion, she inspired in return nothing but dread or resentment: making thus, by a want of that lenity which is the milk of human kindness, and the bond of society, enemies the most numerous and illiberal by those very talents which, more meekly borne, would have rendered her not merely admired, but adored!

"In proportion, however, as she was thus at war

G

with the world in general, the chosen few who were
honoured with her favour she loved with a zeal all her
own; her heart, liberal, open, and but too daringly
sincere, was fervent in affection, and enthusiastic in
admiration; the friends who were dear to her, she was
devoted to serve, she magnified their virtues till she
thought them of a higher race of beings, she inflamed
her generosity with ideas of what she owed to them,
till her life seemed too small a sacrifice to be refused
for their service."

This analysis is confined within the limitations
imposed by the period in which Fanny Burney lived.
It is concerned wholly with the moral elements in
Mrs. Delvile's nature: no account is taken in it of those
imponderables of temperament and taste which in
reality make so important a contribution to the
composition of personality. But, as far as it goes, it
is very shrewd, and reveals an unusual power to isolate
and sum up the basic elements of character. The lack
of balance in Mrs. Delvile, which made her, in spite
of her virtues, an unpopular figure with the world at
large, is stated with a clear, firm certainty, perceived
with an easy mature worldly-wisdom. Here Fanny
Burney shows the advantages that went along with the
limitations of the eighteenth-century outlook. The
fact that it failed to take in large parts of human
experience gave it all the more time and energy to
concentrate on those aspects it did observe. Fanny
Burney was a woman of the world, though this world
was a little narrow. The average second-class female
novelist in the nineteenth century, nervously aware of
more elements in life than she can get into focus,

retains a youthful uncertainty, a jejune vagueness of vision.

Fanny Burney had one more weapon in her armoury, extremely useful for the presentation of the "courtship" element in her stories; an instinctive delicate perception of the processes of feeling in a young girl's heart. Sensitively she can perceive the significance of the small gesture, the almost imperceptible movement indicating the hidden trend of emotion. How justly she describes Cecilia's gradual discovery that her heart is lost to young Delvile! With what a succession of convincing touches she portrays the scene in which the innocent Evelina, already attached to Lord Orville, is found by him stealing home from an apparently compromising interview with Mr. Macartney!

". . . I have reason to believe Lord Orville, from the parlour-window, saw me tottering along; for, before I had taken five steps, he came out, and hastening to meet me, said, 'I fear you are not well; pray allow me (offering his arm) to assist you.'

" 'No, my Lord', said I, with all the resolution I could assume; yet I was forced to turn away my head to conceal my emotion.

" 'You *must*', said he, with earnestness, 'indeed you must—I am sure you are not well; refuse me not the honour of assisting you'; and, almost forcibly, he took my hand, and drawing it under his arm, obliged me to lean upon him. That I submitted was partly the effect of surprise at an earnestness so uncommon in Lord Orville, and partly, that I did not, just then, dare trust my voice to make any objection.

"When we came to the house, he led me into the

parlour, and to a chair, and begged to know if I would not have a glass of water.

" 'No my Lord, I thank you,' said I, 'I am perfectly recovered'; and, rising, I walked to the window, where for some time I pretended to be occupied in looking at the garden.

"Determined as I was to act honourably by Mr. Macartney, I yet most anxiously wished to be restored to the good opinion of Lord Orville; but his silence, and the thoughtfulness of his air, discouraged me from speaking.

"My situation soon grew disagreeable and embarrassing, and I resolved to return to my chamber till breakfast was ready. To remain longer, I feared, might seem *asking* for his enquiries; and I was sure it would ill become me to be more eager to speak, than he was to hear.

"Just as I reached the door, turning to me hastily, he said, 'Are you going, Miss Anville?'

" 'I am, my Lord,' answered I; yet I stopped.

" 'Perhaps to return to—but I beg your pardon!' He spoke with a degree of agitation that made me readily comprehend he meant to *the garden*; and I instinctively said, 'To my own room, my Lord.' And again, I would have gone; but, convinced by my answer that I understood him, I believe he was sorry for the insinuation: he approached me with a very serious air . . ."

Power of story-telling, of character-drawing, ability to trace the process of feeling—with these gifts why should Fanny Burney not have done better than she did? No doubt it is primarily due to a weakness in the essential quality of her talent. The lack of subtlety in her character-drawing, the impression of thinness she makes as compared with the greatest authors, are symptoms of a fundamental lack of mental distinction. Vivacious though her scene may be, it lacks that peculiar individuality of vision which stamps the work of the great creative novelists. So, we feel, might any clever eighteenth-century lady have described the world, had she possessed a turn for writing. Fanny Burney must inevitably have been a minor novelist, for she had not been endowed with a major talent. This, however, is no reason why she should not have been consistently good at her own level; but she is not even that. Even at her best—even in *Cecilia* and *Evelina*—her work is marred by serious faults. For one thing, she could not make her different talents pull together, fuse them in a harmonious whole. This weakness appears conspicuously in her treatment of character. She had, as we have seen, a talent for analysis and a talent for comic presentation: but she never applies both to the same figures. Her comedy characters—the Branghtons and the Larolles—though vividly dramatised, are shallowly conceived. They talk vivaciously and convincingly, but we are never allowed to penetrate beneath that talk to discover the combination of qualities which went to produce their comic exterior. What they are like we see vividly, but not why they were like that. Mrs. Delvile, on the other hand, is diagnosed but not dramatised. A serious type, unsuitable for presentation in a comic convention, she required a far more subtle talent to make her personality vivid on the stage than was needed for the Branghtons. Fanny Burney did not possess such a talent. Her observation was not intelligent enough to enable her to vitalise a deep complex nature whose demeanour was uncoloured by any obvious idiosyncrasies. The consequence is that, though we understand Mrs. Delvile, we never "see" her.

Fanny Burney's books also suffer from the fact that she does not stay within the limitations of her talent. She could have been pretty certain of success if she had only sought to show her reader what a young lady could see: her view of the social scene, her vision of her own heart and its emotions. But she refused to be bound down in this way; in the Madame Duval and Captain Mirvan episodes in *Evelina* she attempts the brutal masculine farce of Smollett: in the Macartney episodes she has a try at tragic drama involving suicide and despair. Fanny Burney, in fact, frequently commits the novelist's greatest sin; she goes outside her true creative range. It was not altogether her fault. The Fielding formula for novel-writing was not a fully matured instrument; it had not solved the problem of reconciling form with fact. In order to give unity and pattern to his realistic panorama of contemporary life Fielding had imposed on it an artificial symmetrical plot copied from that stage comedy in which he had served his apprenticeship as a writer, centring upon a hero and heroine and consisting of a formal intrigue which solves itself neatly in a happy ending.

Where Fielding failed Fanny Burney was not likely to succeed. Her plots are clumsy as well as improbable. To what extraordinary lengths and improbabilities is she forced to go to prevent Cecilia marrying Delvile before the end of the last volume! Moreover, the fact that she imposed a stagey plot on a realistic picture of life involved her in all sorts of material outside her range; and unluckily she was not so powerful and creative an artist as to be able to sweep the reader away so irresistibly that he overlooks her lapses. Indeed, she is hardly an artist at all in the fullest sense of the word. The novel to her was not the expression of an imaginative conception, but merely a means of recording her observations of the world, which she organised into an artificial unity by using any convention of story-writing she found to her hand. Only if she had lived in an age that had presented her ready-made with a thoroughly sound model for a plot, could she have achieved consistently good work. As it was, she was a victim of any influence that crossed her path. *Evelina*, her first book, reveals her at her best and her worst. There is a peculiar charm exhaling from this first fresh sparkling gush of her talent. The Branghton scenes show her comedy at its brightest; Evelina's relation to Orville reveals Fanny Burney's perception at its most sensitive. Both these strains in her story are conceived well within her range.

Alas, this cannot be said of its other elements. The story of the courtship and the picture of the social scene are incongruously combined first of all with an unsuccessful essay in Smollettian farce—the Captain Mirvan-Madame Duval scenes—and secondly with a melodramatic romance in the manner of the novelist of sensibility, featuring a brother saved at the last moment from suicide by the intervention of a hitherto unknown sister, and a father plunged into repentant tears at the sight of his long-lost and also tearful daughter. By the time she wrote *Cecilia*, Fanny Burney had learnt to prune her books of the wildest of these extravagances. There is no more Smollettian farce, and not so much sentimental melodrama. The plot is conceived in a quieter tone. But in its quiet way it is extremely improbable, turning as it does on the idea that two devoted lovers are prevented from marrying because the young man would have to change his surname to something less aristocratic if he did marry. Moreover, plot and character are not so integrated that one seems directly the result of the other. Here Fanny Burney shows conspicuously her inferiority to Jane Austen: she imposes her plot on a picture of life; the action does not arise inevitably from the situation. The Monckton intrigue, for instance, is nothing but a piece of machinery invented to keep the story going.

Furthermore, her prejudiced, enthusiastic, feminine spirit had only escaped from one influence to fall under another. Since she wrote *Evelina* no less a person than Dr. Johnson himself had taken notice of her. She had read his wonderful books with absorbed awe; and now she had begun to shape her own unpretentious talent on his august model. Alas, Dr. Johnson was no better example to her than Smollett. Dr. Johnson was a professional moralist: Fanny Burney thought that she ought to be one too; with the result that she proclaims insistently the moral of her story instead of letting it emerge tacitly from the action. Worse still, the easy colloquial speech of *Evelina* is translated into stately "Johnsonese"—all abstractions and polysyllables and antitheses—a magnificent instrument in Johnson's own hands but comically inappropriate as an expression of Fanny Burney's homely and sociable little personality. All the same, *Cecilia* is the most sustainedly successful of her books; though it lacks the dewy freshness of

Evelina, it maintains a steadier level and reveals a deeper insight into character. *Camilla* and *The Wanderer* written some years after show a decline in every respect. The moralism is more aggressive than ever, and the language more stilted; even the comedy is by comparison fatigued and laboured. Whatever Jane Austen may say in its defence, *Camilla* has sunk from the noble stature of a novel to the mean stature of a tract.

No—Fanny Burney was not an artist, she was not even an efficient craftsman; she approached her work without understanding the capacities either of her own talent or of the form which she had chosen. Responsive and undiscriminating, she lay open to any literary influence that came her way; with the consequence that the harmony of her work, even at its best, is jarred by the introduction of incongruous elements.

Yet she deserves an honourable place in the history of English literature. In her first two books, at any rate, the flame of her creative talent still burns bright enough to keep the whole alive and delightful: and her influence on the course of the novel is yet more important than her achievement. She was the first writer to detect how it might be possible to combine the methods of Richardson and Fielding. *Cecilia*, in particular, is both a novel of analysis and a comic picture of social life. Fanny Burney had not a strong enough talent herself to fuse the two with complete success. For that the English novel had to wait for Jane Austen. Still, it is a credit to anyone to have suggested an idea to Jane Austen. Nor did Fanny Burney's influence stop there. The feminisation of the Fielding type of novel was to prove a momentous step in the history of English literature. From the next century onwards novels were written largely by women and, still more largely, for women. Women have remained passionately interested both in the drama of respectable courtship and the varieties of the social scene. In consequence, a huge proportion of the novels published in the nineteenth century took as their subject a picture of a society seen through the clear, unsophisticated eyes of a young girl freshly launched into it, and grouped round the story of her courtship. Such stories indeed are written still. They are all Fanny Burney's children.

JANE AUSTEN

JANE AUSTEN

JANE Austen, it would appear, did not take her work over-seriously. Hers was no career of solemn and solitary self-dedication. Neat, elegant and sociable, she spent most of her day sitting in the drawing-room of the parsonage which was her home, sewing and gossiping. From time to time, it is said, she would begin to laugh, and then, stepping across to the writing-table, she would scribble a few lines on a sheet of paper. But if visitors called she slipped the pages under the blotter; when the pages had accumulated into a story, she let it lie for years in a drawer unread. And when at last it did emerge to the public gaze, she refused in the slightest degree to modify the conventional order of her life to suit with the character of a professional authoress. As for the applause of posterity, she seems never to have given it a moment's thought: it was no part of her sensible philosophy to worry about admiration that she would not live to enjoy.

Yet one hundred and nineteen years have passed since her death, and yearly the applause of posterity has grown louder. There are those who do not like her; as there are those who do not like sunshine or unselfishness. But the very nervous defiance with which they shout their dissatisfaction shows that they know they are a despised minority. All discriminating critics admire her books, most educated readers enjoy them; her fame, of all English novelists, is the most secure.

These are interesting facts. But they are not really surprising. Success in the art of letters is not so exclusively the affair of tension and temperament that some people seem to fancy. It is strangely enough an affair of art. The most successful writer is he who obeys most strictly the laws which govern the art of his choice. And of all those who have chosen the novel none has been more careful to keep its laws than Jane Austen. It is this that gives her her advantage over other English novelists. She was not the most talented, she did not write about the most sensational topics; but as a master of her craft she outshines them all. And when we turn to analyse our admiration for her it is the triumphs of her craft that first strike us.

To begin with we notice that she obeys the first rule of all imaginative composition, that she stays within the range of her imaginative inspiration. A work of art is born of the union of the artist's experience and his imagination. But only certain aspects of his experience stir a deep enough response in his personality to generate his imaginative spark: only when it is inspired by them does his work have artistic life. It is his first obligation therefore to choose themes within the range of this experience. Now Jane Austen's imaginative range was in some respects a very limited one. It was, in the first place, confined to human beings in their personal relations. Man in relation to God, to politics, to abstract ideas, passed her by: it was only when she saw him with his family and his neighbours that her creative impulse began to stir to activity. She sees Mrs. Brown not as a soul or as a citizen but only as the wife of Mr. Brown. Her view was further limited by the fact that in general she looked at Mrs. Brown in one perspective, the satiric. Jane Austen was a comedian. Her first literary impulse was humorous; and to the end of her life humour was an integral part of her creative process: as her imagination starts to function a smile begins to spread itself across her features. And the smile is the signature on the finished work. It is the angle of her satiric vision, the light of her wit that gives its peculiar glitter and proportion to her picture of the world.

All this meant that she could only be successful with themes that turned on personal relationships and were susceptible in some degree of satiric treatment. Jane Austen, it is her triumph, realised this. She was once asked—and by no less a person than the librarian of the Prince Regent—to write a historical novel about the fortunes of the House of Coburg. But she refused this majestic proposal on the ground that it would be unwise for her to leave her "small square, two inches, of ivory". And, except in a few minor episodes, she never did leave it. All her stories turn on personal relationships, between friends, between parents and children, between men and women in love—and they turn on nothing else at all. She was equally careful to choose themes with satirical implications. She lived through the French Revolution and the Napoleonic Wars, but no shadow of their storm is permitted to confuse the firm bright clarity of her vision. There are no adventures in her books, no abstract ideas, no romantic reveries, no death scenes. Nor does she give much space to the impressions of the senses. This was from no incapacity on her part. The delicate glimpses of landscape that make soft the background of *Persuasion*, the squalid interior of Captain Price's home at Portsmouth where

Fanny's eyes "could only wander from the walls marked by her father's head to . . . the tea-board never thoroughly clean, the cups and saucers wiped in streaks, the milk a mixture of motes floating in thin blue", show that she could paint for the eye with perfect certainty if she had wanted. But satire, like Blake's tear, is an intellectual thing, a critical comment on life. And the impressions of the senses are con, not by critical comment, but by direct record. To interpolate many such records into a comedy will disperse its comic atmosphere. Jane Austen avoided them.

She avoided jarring characters too. Two-thirds of her dramatis personae are regular comic character-parts like Mr. Collins or Mrs. Allen. And even those figures with whom she is most in sympathy, even her heroines, are almost all touched with the comic spirit. Two of them, Emma and Elizabeth Bennet, are a great deal cleverer than most heroines of fiction; one of them, Anne Elliot, is very good. But all three are flesh and blood workaday creatures, able to laugh, if not to be laughed at. Only once, in *Mansfield Park*, did Jane Austen try another type; and she failed. The main lines of Fanny Price's character are admirably conceived, and treasures of subtle observation are poured out on her. But the innocent romantic sweetness, the lovely youthful austerity, which should have been her charm, cannot be conveyed in a comedy vein. So that when she comes to describe them Jane Austen's hand for once falters. Fanny is a little wooden, a little charmless, and rather a prig.

Indeed, youthful romance, unless she could laugh at it, was not within Jane Austen's province. The nature of her talent imposed a third limitation on her; it made her unable to express impulsive emotion directly. She surveyed her creatures with too detached an irony for her to identify herself with them sufficiently to voice their unthinking gushes of feeling. On the few occasions she tried she becomes self-conscious, unreal and, incredible to relate, rather absurd. "The evergreen," exclaims Fanny, rhapsodising in a Wordsworthian moment over the Mansfield plantations, "how beautiful, how welcome, how wonderful the evergreen." But such lapses are rare. Generally Jane Austen is as artful in avoiding the occasion for them as in everything else. She traces brilliantly the effect of emotion, the way it heats a situation, modifies character; but she expresses it only by implication. Her plots turn on love, but only one of her lovers, the self-controlled Mr. Knightley, do we hear declare his passion. We are shown exactly how Anne Elliot's love of nature coloured her mood, but she is never allowed to tell us of it in person.

Jane Austen's natural range was further bounded by the limitations imposed by circumstances. No author, except a fantasist, can make anything living of worlds of which he is not personally experienced. The world of Jane Austen's experience was a very small one. She was a woman in an age when women were forbidden by convention from moving in any society except that in which they were born: and the class she was born in, that of the smaller English gentry, was the one most enslaved to convention. But she kept to it. Her stories all take place in England, all in one class. Further, she is one of the few women novelists who have accepted the limitations of their sex. She never describes

H

a scene in which no woman is present; her heroes are shown to us, fragmentarily, and with character and motives in part unexplained, as they appeared to the girls with whom they came in contact. Here as elsewhere she is true almost uniformly to the first rule of literary art, she excludes from her books all aspects of life that cannot pass through the crucible of her imagination. So that every inch of her book is vital.

She is not only true to the rules of literary art in general; she is also true to the particular laws that govern the art of the novel. The novelist has a more complex task than the poet. For he sets out to give a picture of the world as it is. And this confronts him with two problems. First he has to reconcile reality with imagination. Like all works of art his book should be an expression of his personality; but it must also be a convincing record of facts. And he can only attain the highest success if he satisfies both these conditions equally. Many great novelists do not. *Jane Eyre* is drenched through with the lurid element of Charlotte Brontë's imagination; but as a picture of a governess's life in the 1840's it is, to say the least of it, unconvincing. Trollope on the other hand tends to present us with a mere accurate photograph untinged by the colour of an individual vision. Now Jane Austen's imagination was, as we have seen, a comedian's imagination. Her problem is to draw a true picture of life which should also amuse us. And in the masterpieces of her maturity, in *Emma* and *Persuasion*, she succeeds perfectly. She paints the surface of English life with a meticulous and Dutch accuracy; Miss Bates is a bore exactly like a hundred bores we fly from every day. Only—we find ourselves hanging on her words; by a delightful miracle

she has been made entertaining. Jane Austen could per-
form similar miracles upon even less promising material.
Examine the account in *Emma* of how the news of
Mrs. Churchill's death was received at Highbury.

"It was felt as such things must be felt. Everybody
had a degree of gravity and sorrow; tenderness towards
the departed, solicitude for the surviving friends; and,
in a reasonable time, curiosity to know where she would
be buried. Goldsmith tells us that when lovely woman
stoops to folly, she has nothing to do but to die; and
when she stoops to be disagreeable, it is equally to be
recommended as a clearer of ill fame. Mrs. Churchill,
after being disliked at least twenty-five years, was now
spoken of with compassionate allowances. In one point
she was fully justified. She had never been admitted
before to be seriously ill. The event acquitted her of
all the fancifulness and all the selfishness of imaginary
complaints."

Here is no comic distortion of sad reality. This, we
know, is exactly how the news of such a death would
be received by such people. Yet we cannot read it
without laughing.

Even when Jane Austen is not out primarily to make
us laugh she never wholly leaves the realm of comedy.
She describes Anne's love for Wentworth with an
exquisite sympathy; but her sympathy does not blind
her to whatever ironical implications it may have.
Anne is sure that when Lady Russell looks out of the
carriage, in which they are driving, it is to gaze
at Wentworth. Jane Austen notes with amusement
that in reality it is to see what is in the shops. However

intractable her material may seem to be, she manages to tinge it with a comic tone.

It is partly due to the judgment with which she chooses her angle of vision. She puts herself in a position in which the humorous aspects of her subject stand out most obviously, so that by only setting out the facts in their unemphasised sobriety she can make them amusing. Mrs. Churchill's death had no doubt its solemn aspects, but they were not noticeable from the point of view from which Jane Austen looks at it. Comedy is also implicit in the manner in which she tells her story. Her irony, her delicate ruthless irony is of the very substance of her style. It never obtrudes itself; sometimes it only glints out in a turn of phrase. But it is never absent for more than a paragraph; and her most straightforward piece of exposition is tart with its perfume. Mrs. Bennet "was a woman of mean understanding, little information, and uncertain temper. When she was discontented she fancied herself nervous. The business of her life was to get her daughters married; its solace was visiting and news". From a serious point of view this is an admirable summary of Mrs. Bennet's character. Tolstoy himself could not have stated it more completely. But Tolstoy would have stated it without a smile; while every word of Jane Austen's, every curt rhythm, every neat antithesis betrays she is not speaking with a straight face. By the mere tone of her voice she sets drab reality dancing and sparkling with the sunlight of her comic vision.

Her troubles are not over when she has satisfied the rival claims of fact and imagination. Here we come to the second problem with which the nature of his material confronts the novelist. A work of art is an orderly unity; life is a heterogeneous tangle. The writer has to devise a form for his inspiration which will at once please us as an artistic pattern and give us a convincing impression of disorderly reality. In addition to reconciling fact and imagination he must reconcile fact and form. It is a hard task: and, it cannot be said that Jane Austen always succeeded in it. In *Northanger Abbey* and *Sense and Sensibility* she sacrifices fact to form. The character of Edward Ferrars, the eccentric conduct of General Tilney, these are too palpably pieces of machinery invented to fit the exigencies of the plot. In *Mansfield Park* she sacrifices form to fact. The original design of the book obviously intended Henry Crawford to fill the rôle of villain. But as she works Jane Austen's creative power gets out of control, Henry Crawford comes to life as a sympathetic character; and under the pressure of his personality the plot takes a turn, of which the only logical conclusion is his marriage with the heroine, Fanny. Jane Austen was not one to be put upon by her creatures in this way. In the last three chapters she violently wrenches the story back into its original course: but only at the cost of making Henry act in a manner wholly inconsistent with the rest of his character.

At her best, however, she keeps the balance between fact and form as no other English novelist has ever done. She neither twists reality to fit a logical scheme like Henry James, nor like Scott lets life tumble pell-mell about the reader's head in indeterminate confusion. Her stories are meticulously integrated; not a character, not an episode but makes its necessary contribution to the development of the plot. Only, we do not notice it. The scaffolding is so artfully overlaid with the foliage of her invention that it seems a free growth. She makes her incidents so natural, endows her characters with so independent a reality, that it is possible to read about them without ever realising that they are part of a scheme at all. Even if we do realise it we are half in doubt as to whether it is an intentional scheme. The picture she presents to us seems no calculated composition but rather a glimpse of life itself; life caught at a moment when its shifting elements have chanced to group themselves into a temporary symmetry. *Emma* and *Pride and Prejudice* are as logically constructed as a detective story; yet they give us all the sense of spontaneous life we get from a play of Chekhov.

Persuasion is less impeccably designed: Mrs. Smith, like Edward Ferrars, is a bit of lifeless machinery. But it is its author's greatest formal achievement. For in it she gives her story not only a dramatic but also a spiritual unity. Its subject is love, the constant love renounced from an unwise prudence, that Anne Elliot feels for Wentworth. And every episode of the story refers to this subject. The rash happy marriage of the Crofts, the love, enduring through hardship, of the Harvilles, the inconstancy of Benwick and Louisa Musgrove—all these, by contrast or similarity, illustrate Anne's situation: now in the major key, now in the minor, now simply, now with variations, they repeat the main theme of the symphony. Even the tender autumnal weather in which most of the action takes place echoes and symbolises the prevailing mood of the story. Such singleness of structure gives *Persuasion* an emotional concentration unattainable by any other means. Yet this structure is not emphasised in such a way as to destroy the illusion of every-day reality. The reader never feels that Benwick and the rest of them are put in to play their part in the harmony, but just because they happened to be features of the bit of actual life Jane Austen has chosen to describe. By a supreme feat of dexterity she has managed to compose a symphony on the theme of love, which is also a realistic story of ordinary human beings.

Jane Austen then is the only English novelist who has managed fully to satisfy the three essential requirements of her art, the only one who has solved all three of its major problems. Certainly there is no reason to wonder at her reputation. And yet one cannot help feeling that something more is needed to account for it. Mere technical accomplishment is not enough to explain the impression she makes on us. After all, a work of art may be perfect technically and yet be a minor work, a porcelain vase, an ormolu snuff-box. And Jane Austen, so far from being a manufacturer of literary snuff-boxes, is one of the few supreme novelists of the world. The absorbing, searching interest she awakes in the mind—so that one turns to her again and again and always finds something new to think about—is one only stirred by works of major art. Her books—it is the second reason for their enduring popularity—have a universal significance.

This is due in the first place to the sheer strength of their author's talent; to the fact that she is endowed in the highest degree with the one essential gift of the novelist, the power to create living characters. It is true that she only draws them in their private aspect. But this is not a superficial aspect. A man's relation to his wife and children is at least as important a part of his life as his relation to his beliefs and career; and reveals him as fundamentally. Indeed, it reveals his moral side more fundamentally. If you want to know about a man's talents you should see him in society, if you want to know about his temper you should see him at home. Nor is Jane Austen's view rendered less fundamental by the fact that she shows him as a rule not in moments of crisis but in the trivial incidents of every day. Life is made up of little things, and human nature reveals itself in them as fully as in big ones: a picnic shows up selfishness, kindness, vanity, sincerity, as much as a battle. Only you must have the faculty to discern them. Jane Austen had. Her eye for the surface of personality is unerring. Not Dickens himself can visualise outward idiosyncrasies of his creatures more vividly, their manner, their charm, their tricks of speech.

But unlike Dickens, Jane Austen also realises the psychological organism that underlies speech and manner. She is not content just to dash down her intuitive impressions of people; her lucid knife-edged mind was always at work penetrating beneath such impressions to discern their cause, discover the principles of her subject's conduct, the peculiar combination of qualities that go to make up his individuality. And she shows us surface peculiarities always in relation to these essentials. The consequence is she does not need to present man involved in major catastrophes. If for once her plot does entail her portraying her characters in moments of serious crisis, she can do it perfectly. Louisa Musgrove, skipping down the steps of the Cobb at Lyme, trips and falls apparently lifeless. With acute insight Jane Austen illustrates the way the rest of the party react to this disaster: how the egotistic Mary Musgrove is absorbed in her egotistic agitation, how the unrestrained Henrietta collapses, how Wentworth's sympathetic imagination conjures up at once the effect of the news on Louisa's parents, how Anne alone, unselfish, self-controlled Anne, keeps her head. But though we admire Jane Austen's insight it tells us nothing new about these people; the uneventful walks and dinner parties where we have already seen them have revealed their disposition so fully that we could have foretold how they would behave.

Indeed, Jane Austen's understanding of the moral nature of man is, within the limitations of her experience, complete. She may not have known all that the people of her world thought and fancied, but she knew exactly which was good and which bad, discriminated exactly the individual shade of their goodness or badness, exactly perceived how it showed itself in their behaviour. Nothing escapes her, nothing baffles her, nothing deceives her. However slight its manifestation, however muffled by convention or disguised by personal charm, unfailingly she detects the essential quality of character. The Miss Bertrams

"joined to beauty and brilliant acquirements a manner naturally easy, and carefully formed to general civility and obligingness. . . . Their vanity was in such good order, that they seemed to be quite free from it, and gave themselves no airs; while the praises attending such behaviour . . . served to strengthen them in believing they had no faults".

Only two sentences: but they make us understand the Miss Betrams completely.

Such penetration enabled her to elucidate far more complex characters than most novelists. The young ladies who play the chief rôles in her stories are more intricately conceived than those of any English novelist before George Eliot. Emma is a complex mixture of vanity, wilfulness, and fundamental generous feeling; Mary Crawford a complex mixture of sympathy and selfishness, shallowness and common sense. Each of these qualities is precisely defined for us. Yet the result is no impersonal analysed psychological case like those which make dreary the stories of some of our distinguished contemporaries. The vivid intensity of Jane Austen's vision fuses them together into a single breathing moving human being. Emma and Mary Crawford are equally real as personalities and as characters.

Not less acute is Jane Austen's insight into the processes of the heart: the minute symptoms—half-said word, instinctive imperceptible movement—by which people betray an emotion. We *know* that Darcy is still in love with Elizabeth though he has not spoken to her all the evening because "he brought back his coffee cup himself" to the table where she was pouring out: we realise Anne's complete absorption in Wentworth as we watch her move almost involuntarily to the table at which he has been writing the moment he has left the room. And Jane Austen can follow through its most hidden and discursive windings the course by which feeling expresses itself in the mind. Fanny Price, agonised with jealousy, is kept waiting for her ride while Edmund is taking her rival for a turn on her horse. She does not admit she is jealous even to herself, but her irritation vents itself in a sudden spurt of indignation at the inconsiderate way they are tiring the animal.

"She began to think it rather hard upon the mare to have such double duty; if she were forgotten, the poor mare should be remembered."

This quotation illustrates another of Jane Austen's particular merits, her impartiality. It is the most important consequence of her consistently ironical attitude that she never idealises. Her most virtuous characters have their faults. And, what is more striking, she shows us how these faults are integral to their natures. Fanny is unselfish and high-minded. But Jane Austen perceives that these same virtues bring along with them, as a necessary corollary, certain weaknesses; that Fanny's very habit of self-abnegation led her, if for once she had a selfish feeling, to disguise it from herself; that her very strictness of principle was liable to make her unjust to her more frivolous rival.

Jane Austen is equally honest about the characters she did not like. She loathed Mrs. Norris—who could do otherwise?—and thought her far more odious than harmless silly Mrs. Price. But she sees that the same meddling energy which made her so disagreeable would have fitted her far better than Mrs. Price to cope with the difficulties of a poor sailor's wife with a large family. And she says so. This impartiality gives her characters volume: they are not brilliantly drawn silhouettes, but solid, three-dimensional figures, who can be looked at from several sides.

And there is a huge number of them. Jane Austen's

range of character is very large. She painted on such a narrow canvas that people have not always realised this. But a wide canvas does not necessarily mean a wide range. Thackeray painted on a vast one, but his range of characters is small. For he always repeats them; his good women are all pictures of the same person in a different dress. Jane Austen's good women, Anne Elliot, Elinor Dashwood, Fanny Price, are all different. In her six books she never repeats a single character. The snobbishness of the Rev. Mr. Collins is unlike that of the Rev. Mr. Elton: Isabella Thorpe and Lucy Steele are both calculating flirts but not the same sort of calculating flirt: there is all the difference in the world between the vulgarity of Mrs. Bennet and the vulgarity of Mrs. Jennings. Out of her small parsonage house Jane Austen's gay wand conjures innumerable troops of unique individuals.

So comprehensive and so searching a view of human nature inevitably invests her achievement with a universal character. For all that she paints the nineteenth century English scene with so sedulous an accuracy, this accuracy is an unimportant part of the impression that she makes. *Mansfield Park* does not, like *Cranford*, appeal to us first of all by its period charm: we do not remember Mr. Elton as we remember Archdeacon Grantly because he is such a true picture of an English clergyman. He could turn into a Scotch minister and we should still recognise him. For he lives not in virtue of his likeness to national character but to essential human nature. Essential human nature—this is always Jane Austen's preoccupation. Her characters are universal types. Miss Bates is the type of all bores, Mrs. Elton the type of all pushing vulgarians, Marianne

Dashwood the type of all undisciplined romantics;
when Mr. Woodhouse tells us that his grandchildren
are "all remarkably clever . . . they will come and stand
by my chair and say 'grandpapa, can you give me a bit
of string?' " he sums up the fatuous fondness of all
grandparents; when Mr. Darcy says "I have been
selfish all my life in practice but not in principle" he
confesses the weakness of high-minded dominating
males in every age and climate. Jane Austen's realistic
English drawing-rooms, like the unfurnished ante-
chambers of French classical drama, are theatres in
which elemental human folly and inconsistency play
out their eternal comedy.

This brings me to the second fact about her work
which gives it a universal character. Like all great
comedians, she satirises in relation to a universal standard of values: her books express a general view of life.
It is the view of that eighteenth-century civilisation of
which she was the last exquisite blossom. One might
call it the moral-realistic view. Jane Austen was
profoundly moral. She thought you lived only to be
good, that it was the first duty of everyone to be sincere,
unselfish and disinterested. But the very seriousness
with which she held this conviction made her think it
imperative to see life realistically. Good notions were to
be acted upon; therefore you could only be sure they
were good if they had passed the test of common sense
and experience. She despised all ideals, however lofty,
that were not practical, all emotions, however soul
stirring, if they did not in fact make for the benefit and
happiness of mankind. Indeed she did not value
emotions as such at all. She reserved some of her most
mischievous mockery for extravagant maternal affection

and sentimental rhapsodising over nature. Love itself, though she understood its workings admirably, did not rouse her enthusiasm unless it was justified by reason, disciplined by self-control. She had little sympathy for romantic imprudence or credulous good nature; she was impatient of people with hearts of gold and heads of wood. And though she was not a slave to worldly considerations she thought it a mistake to overlook them entirely. It was wrong to marry for money, but it was silly to marry without it. Nor should one lightly break with convention. Only fools imagined they could live happily in the world without paying attention to what its inhabitants thought.

Further, her realism made her think it foolish to worry about evils one could not prevent. Life was clearly an imperfect affair at the best; but it had to be lived. And a sensible man, except in so far as it interfered with the performance of his duty, concentrated on life's pleasant aspects. "How horrible it is", she writes about a battle in the Peninsular War, "to have so many killed, and what a blessing that one cares for none of them." This robust attitude to the ills inevitable to mortality, is rare to-day—which is a pity. It is the only one in which a man of principle can live through troubled times without growing intolerably depressed.

This rational sense of the value of happiness is the origin of her third standard of judgment—taste. As much an artist in life as in her work, Jane Austen recognised that how you live is only second in importance to what you live for, that life is a question of form as well as of content. To be completely satisfactory as a human being you need to be not only good and sensible but also well-mannered and cultivated. For intelligence and refinement add to the pleasantness of life. She did not admire noble savages or rough diamonds or genial slovenly vulgarians. If you could not manage to be good there was some merit in being good-mannered. Mansfield Park was not morally superior to Fanny's Portsmouth home, but it was preferable for "its elegance, propriety, regularity and harmony". It is this sensibility to the value of form which makes Jane Austen's view of life so much more convincing than those of the Victorians who followed her. There is nothing puritanical or provincial about it, it recognises that body and mind have their claims as well as soul, it is a civilised philosophy for civilised people.

And it permeates every aspect of her work. Not that she is a deliberate preacher using the novel as a means to teach her gospel. In a sense she was too confident in its truth. What was the point, she felt, in expounding principles which must be obvious to any rational person. Besides the spectacle of human ineptitude amused her too much for her to have any great wish to put an end to it. She wrote primarily just to entertain. But her view of life was so fundamental to her personality that her every imaginative conception is related to it. Not one of her characters, however farcical or however delightful, but is brought to trial before the triple bar of taste, sense and virtue; and if they fail to give satisfaction on any one of these counts, smiling but relentless she passes sentence on them. Her sense of justice is exquisite and implacable; neither pity nor anger can make it swerve from its course; she is never vindictive and never sentimental; she makes no exceptions in deference to public opinion or to her personal feelings. Mary Crawford is extremely sensible and as charming as Elizabeth Bennet herself. But she cannot face marrying a clergyman: she is condemned. Marianne Dashwood had no such worldly weakness; and she is also charming. But she is the prey of romantic illusions; and for this she too receives her punishment.

Jane Austen applies the standards of taste equally ruthlessly. Miss Bates was a bore but she was also a kind old spinster with an excellent heart. If Dickens had described her, her heart would have shed a softening halo over her boringness. Jane Austen does every justice to her good qualities; but she makes her as boring as she possibly can. Not grief itself can shield a character from the death-ray of her fastidiousness.

"Mrs. Musgrove was of a comfortable, substantial size, infinitely more fitted by nature to express good cheer and good humour than tenderness and sentiment; . . . Captain Wentworth should be allowed some credit for the self-command with which he attended to her large fat sighings over the destiny of a son whom alive nobody had cared for. Personal size and mental sorrow have certainly no necessary proportions. A large bulky figure has as good a right to be in deep affliction as the most graceful set of limbs in the world. But, fair or not fair, there are unbecoming conjunctions, which reason will patronise in vain—which taste cannot tolerate— which ridicule will seize."

Jane Austen is not heartless, she sympathises fully with whatever is genuine in Mrs. Musgrove's sorrow; but she sees there is something absurd about her even in lamentation. And she points it out.

Her outlook expresses itself as much in general structure as in detail. Her stories are not just strings of incident and character knit together by a plot for the sake of convenience. Each is built round a theme; and this theme illustrates some aspect of her view of life. They divided themselves into three groups. *Northanger Abbey* and *Sense and Sensibility* satirise that romantic philosophy which was sweeping the world in the early nineteenth century. Romanticism, referring all its judgments as it did to the guidance of the instinctive movements of heart and imagination, was profoundly alien to Jane Austen. In *Northanger Abbey* she laughs at its superficial aspects. Catherine Morland is a simple girl who is always making a fool of herself because she expects life to be like the romantic novels which are her favourite reading. *Sense and Sensibility* is a more fundamental attack. Elinor Dashwood guides her conduct by reason, Marianne by the impulses of her enthusiastic nature: the story shows how experience proves Elinor right and Marianne wrong. *Emma* and *Pride and Prejudice* deal with more personal questions. *Pride and Prejudice* exhibits the folly of trusting to first impressions uncorrected by mature observation. Elizabeth Bennet is misled by the immediate agreeability of the one and the haughty formality of the other, into liking Wickham and disliking Darcy: the action describes how further knowledges teaches her to reverse these opinions. *Emma*, Jane Austen's profoundest comedy, satirises the self-deceptions of vanity. Emma is a clever woman whose confidence in her own cleverness blinds her to reality. She spends her life in trying to rearrange the lives of others; but her plans when put into practice only reveal her failure to understand either the dispositions of the

I

people she is dealing with, or the true nature of her own feelings and motives. *Mansfield Park* and *Persuasion* are more serious. Though they are composed within the limitations of Jane Austen's comic convention, their subjects are not so essentially satirical. *Mansfield Park* contrasts worldliness with unworldliness; the story illustrates the superiority of the disinterested Fanny and Edmund to the crude worldly Bertrams on the one hand, and on the other hand, more subtly, to the clever worldly Crawfords. *Persuasion* is about love. How far should love be restrained by prudential considerations? It is a different sort of subject from that of her other books; and the pensive sympathy, with which she discusses it, betrays a softening of her prevailing mood. Sad experience has taught her that the problems of the heart are too momentous to be decided with the unhesitating confidence of her high-spirited youth. But the standard by which she decides them remains the same. Anne is declared mistaken in her early renunciation of Wentworth, not because love should override all other considerations, but because Wentworth was virtuous and industrious enough for a reasonable woman to risk poverty with him.

This considered intellectual foundation means that the interest of Jane Austen's books is far more serious than their surface appearance would lead us to expect. These spinsters and curates have the universal significance of the scheme of values in whose light they are presented to us: these quiet comedies of country life propound fundamental problems of human conduct. In every age, every country, people must decide whether they will direct their lives by feeling or reason, decide how much importance they should attach to considerations of prudence or worldly advantage; in every age and country, people are misled by first impressions, deceived by over-confidence in their own powers. The issues between Elinor and Marianne are the issues between Rousseau and Dr. Johnson: the errors that are the undoing of Emma have undone many statesmen and social reformers; though the setting and costumes of *Mansfield Park* may be those of *Cranford*, its drama expresses a criticism of life as comprehensive as that of *Madame Bovary*.

Nor does the limited theatre of its presentation impair the power of this criticism. On the contrary, it increases it. It gives it charm. The unique irresistible flavour of her work, its gay astringent buoyancy, its silvery commonsense arises from the unexpected combination of her realistic moralism with the delicate elegance of its setting. Moreover, the fact that she kept so carefully to the only world she knew thoroughly well, meant that she was not distracted by superficial idiosyncrasies, but could penetrate beneath them to perceive its more general significance. *Emma* is universal just because it is narrow; because it confines itself to the range of Jane Austen's profoundest vision.

For it is a profound vision. There are other views of life and more extensive; concerned as it is exclusively with personal relationships, it leaves out several important aspects of experience. But on her own ground Jane Austen gets to the heart of the matter; her graceful unpretentious philosophy, founded as it is on an unwavering recognition of fact, directed by an unerring perception of moral quality, is as impressive as those of the most majestic novelists. Myself I find it more impressive. If I were in doubt as to the wisdom of one of my actions I should not consult Flaubert or Dos-toievsky. The opinion of Balzac or Dickens would carry little weight with me: were Stendhal to rebuke me, it would only convince me I had done right: even in the judgment of Tolstoy I should not put complete confidence. But I should be seriously upset, I should worry for weeks and weeks, if I incurred the disapproval of Jane Austen.

TURGENEV

TURGENEV

SOME time towards the second half of the last
century there appeared in the bookshops of Western
Europe the translation of a novel by Ivan Turgenev.
It was the first work by an important Russian author
so to be translated; and the impression made was tremendous. In Paris—then the centre of all that was most
alive in the world of art and letters—fastidious and
intelligent critics vied with one another in praise:
Flaubert, the most fastidious and intelligent of the lot,
even went so far as to say "This gigantic Scythian has
surpassed us all". Turgenev, however, proved no
isolated phenomenon. During the years that followed
his entry on to the stage of Western Europe, he was
succeeded by that of other Scythians not less gigantic.
And the impression made by two of them in particular,
Tolstoy and Dostoievsky, was so dazzling as to dim for a
time that made by the first star; so that, in general, the
reputation of Turgenev has been overshadowed by that
of his two tremendous compatriots.

It is natural that it should be. In some important
respects they are more impressive. Turgenev is not
built on the same scale, he is not so gigantic a giant.
He lacks Tolstoy's sheer breadth of vision, embracing
as it does equally in its view peasants and princes, duck-
shooting and religious doubt. Nor has he Dostoievsky's
power to illuminate with an equal intensity of spiritual
insight, the depths of criminal degradation and the
heights of religious ecstasy. Beside *War and Peace* or

The Possessed, Turgenev's novels look a little pale. Yet if we give him time, if we let our eyes grow accustomed to his lower scale of tone, his spell begins to work on us; and we shut the book not at all so sure that Turgenev is inferior to his majestic brother authors. For, as might be expected, Flaubert had ground for his sweeping statement. Turgenev has his own merits—merits denied to Tolstoy and Dostoievsky—that give him a secure place among the world's supreme novelists.

Nor is he so wholly different from other Russians as might appear. He is more like them than he is like Fielding or Balzac. Common nationality, common civilisation, imposes on its children a common outlook. Turgenev's imagination works on the world of human beings and their relationships, which is always the novelist's subject matter, in what is to a Western eye a distinctively Russian way. It combines, that is to say, as that of other novelists do not, an extreme realism with an extreme spirituality. Russian novels are both more realistic and more religious than other novels. There is no doubt about their realism. From Lermontov to Chekov, Russian writers are out to describe experience exactly as it is. Apparently they never feel the temptation to reject or modify any aspect of the reality they are describing for artistic reasons. They do not tamper with the facts in order to make their story more shapely or more pleasing or more dramatic. Nor do they intensify their effect by steeping the sober facts of life in a glow of fantasy. Dostoievsky writes novels about religious experience, like Shorthouse : unlike Shorthouse, however, he does not actually bring the supernatural on the stage. *War and Peace* is an historical novel like *Waverley*, but Tolstoy does not explore the picturesque and the romantic aspects of the past as Scott does. Russian literature, like other literatures, has given us lovable heroines, but they are never idealised pictures of femininity. The heroines are described as unsentimentally and with as careful regard for realistic truth as everybody else. Indeed, it is a little disconcerting at first to find their creators carefully pointing out that some charming girl has "a thick nose" or "a muddy complexion" or "a small wart on the chin". Equally their plots are true to fact. Chekov's stories, compared to the short stories of his Western contemporaries, have no plot in the conventional sense of the word. Beginning in the middle of a situation, they stop as often as not abruptly and indeterminedly, like an episode in real life.

Yet though the Russians are realistic they are not materialistic. Here again they differ from the writers of the West. Western realists, Maupassant and Zola, represent human beings as ruled and conditioned by economic and physical circumstances. Not so the Russians: for the Christian religion had soaked itself so deeply into every fibre of Russian society, that to Russians, the soul was as unquestioned a fact as the body. Any true picture of reality must include it. Indeed the soul—as must inevitably be the case for a genuine believer—is the picture's most important feature. These realistic stories about generals and civil servants are, first of all, stories about the progress of their souls: these realistically-drawn heroines have always an intense and active spiritual life. No doubt the characters in Russian novels do many of the same things that they do in Western novels; marry, make money, pursue worldly advantage. But these activities are shown always in relation to the central action, the progress of the soul; and their interest lies in how far they affect it. "Will my spirit be satisfied if I marry X?" the Russian heroine asks herself. "Will it help me to lead a good life?" And finally, "What do I mean by good?" It is their preoccupation with these matters which led so many of their first English readers— virtuous, healthy, confident Philistines—to condemn the Russians as introspective. They are introspective as much as anyone is, who is conscious of having a soul, and a duty to it.

This mixture of realism and spirituality is as characteristic of Turgenev as of Tolstoy or Dostoievsky. His books are varied in subject; sketches of peasant life, love stories, one semi-political novel, *Virgin Soil*, two straight studies of character, *Fathers and Children* and *Rudin*. But all are treated from the Russian angle of vision. Turgenev is vigilantly realistic. If he has a plot in the Western sense, as in *The House of Gentlefolk*, it is a strictly probable one, arising logically from character and situation. And his most characteristic books, like *Fathers and Children* and *Rudin* have no such regular plot, but are just a series of apparently insignificant incidents. The characters too are realistically described. They are good and bad, comic and serious, but never artificially divided into heroes and villains, serious parts and comic relief. Nor are they types or symbols; each is carefully individualised, all are described with the same detailed realism.

On the other hand all are related to a spiritual standard. *The House of Gentlefolk*, for example, is the story of a man who, thinking his wife dead, engages himself to a virtuous young girl. The wife returns, and the lovers have to part. This is a more conventional plot than is usual with Turgenev, and could have been treated as a straight love story, passionate and pathetic. For Turgenev, however, the significance of the action lies in its relation to the spiritual health of the hero and heroine. Lavretzky, the hero, hopes that love will redeem his hitherto wasted life. The heroine, Lisa, takes its unhappy end as a sign that it was a love not blessed by God, whose very rapture was a danger, since it led the soul to set itself on things of this world. In expiation she becomes a nun. Turgenev's other stories have a similar sort of significance. Always the characters are in search of spiritual satisfaction, always they are regarded as successful in so far as they attain it.

So far Turgenev's books are like those of the other Russians. After this we find a difference. The Russian point of view rests upon an acceptance of the Christian interpretation of the human predicament. Human life, that is to say, is unsatisfactory in so far as it is out of touch with God. With Tolstoy and Dostoievsky this Christian point of view means an actual profession of Christianity, according to their respective and highly individual interpretations of that faith. With Turgenev not: intellectually he was an agnostic. There might be a God, on the other hand there might not. There might be an after life, he tended to think there was; but he could not say for certain. Human life was a mystery, a brief, inexplicable flash of light between darkness and darkness. Yet Turgenev was not hostile to Christianity. He had been soaked in its tradition too early. Indeed, his reactions to life are more essentially Christian than those of many officially orthodox persons. He describes religious characters with an exquisite sympathy, and his own moral standards are Christian standards. As with Thomas Hardy, another reluctant agnostic, the specific Christian virtues, charity, humility, resignation, are the most beautiful to him. He blesses the meek and pure of heart, those that hunger and thirst after righteousness. Love to him is the fulfilling of the law. Further he has the Christian sense of the congenital frailty and imperfection of human beings. "There was no reproach in her heart; she did not dare to question God's will"; so he says of Elena at that final catastrophe of her life, when the lover for whom she has sacrificed everything, lies dead before her eyes. "She did not ask why He had punished her beyond her gift, if she were guilty. Each of us is guilty, by the fact that he lives; and there is no one so great a benefactor to mankind that he might hope to have a right to live for the service he has done." Once more like Hardy, Turgenev casts a longing, lingering look behind him to that pure bright faith which he had lost. His profoundest book, *Fathers and Children*, ends with a desperate cry of uncertain defiant belief in the possibility of some after-life in which wrong shall be righted and suffering relieved. Bazarov dies; his broken hearted old parents, who had hoped so much for him, come to mourn over his grave.

"Can it be that their prayers, their tears are hopeless? Can it be that love, holy, devoted love is not all-powerful? Ah, no! however passionate, sinning and rebellious is the heart that lies in the grave, yet the flowers growing over it gaze at us serenely and with innocent eyes; telling us of peace—not merely the great peace of indifferent nature—but also of eternal reconciliation, of life without end."

Christian feelings without Christian faith—this about

sums up Turgenev's condition of mind. Inevitably it
makes his picture of life a sad one. Not disagreeably
sad: for there is nothing ugly or mean about it. On the
contrary, Turgenev's picture shows he was peculiarly
responsive to the noble and the beautiful. Unfor-
tunately, however, he was not sure whether they
corresponded to anything permanent in the Universe;
whether in fact human beings were not the creatures of
some ruthless, mechanical, unknown force. Lisa may
become a nun in order to find salvation for her soul—
who knows if salvation, as she means it, exists? Elena
may accept her tragedy as a just chastisement for the sins
of mankind; but perhaps the beauty of her resignation
will be her only reward. When all is said, the significance of human life remains clouded in sad, insoluble
mystery. But this does not make Turgenev love life less.
Indeed, his rapture at its beauty is all the more poignant
because he feels that beauty to be so elusive, so fleeting.
Here we come to the second strain in his prevailing
mood which differentiates it from that of the other
Russian classics. He is much more specifically and
consciously æsthetic in his response to experience. He
looks to beauty for his chief satisfaction in life. Natural
temperament was primarily responsible for this; but
his philosophy or lack of philosophy encouraged him
still further. Beauty was a consolation. When all else
is uncertain, beauty could still make life worth living.
For Turgenev beauty included moral beauty. Here he
separates himself from the professional æsthete of the
West, and reveals the congenital Christianity of his
outlook. Flowers and trees, music and poetry are lovely,
but even lovelier is human virtue. But it is a difference
of degree, not kind. Virtue appealed to Turgenev in

the same way as flowers and music did. His standard of value was fundamentally æsthetic.

So also was his attitude to his work. Unlike most novelists he approaches both his subject-matter and his treatment of it from as æsthetic a point of view as a musician's. It is his æsthetic impulse that makes him write at all. He doesn't want to give us facts, still less to preach a gospel: he simply wants to create something beautiful. Perhaps this accounts for his relative lack of intensity; for it does imply a certain detachment. But it also gives his achievement its unique quality. The fact that he is far more continuously inspired by his sensibility to the beautiful than are most novelists makes the novel in his hands far more consistently a work of art, a work of art in the sense that a sonata of Mozart is. Incidentally, he is one of the few writers who can describe the effect of a work of art convincingly. He succeeds in making us feel that Lemm's sonata in the *House of Gentlefolk*, and the victorious song in the singing match in *The Sportsman's Sketches* were as beautiful as their hearers thought them to be. But Turgenev's æsthetic sensibility shows itself everywhere in his work. In his settings for example: the landscape plays an enormous part in his picture. It is impossible to recall a Turgenev story without evoking in our imagination the Russian scene in which it is set—the birch trees and far horizons and sweeping cornfields, shimmering in the sunshine or shadowy in the pale light of the moon. For a parallel in English literature we have to go to Hardy. But Hardy's use of landscape is different. For him it is a symbol; black Egdon Heath stands for the inhuman forces of nature against which frail mortality struggles in vain. Turgenev's use of landscape is purely æsthetic. The birch tree and the cornfield are just birch tree and cornfield. As much as to Peter Bell, the primrose by the river's brim was, to Turgenev, a simple primrose. But he saw it with so exquisite a precision, such a feeling for its individual quality, that it stirs in us the same sentiment that a real primrose would.

Equally discriminating is Turgenev's appreciation of moral virtue. This appears above all in his heroines. Though subtly different in detail, they are alike in type. Lisa, Marianna, Elena—all are of the same family, simple and single-minded, pure and passionate. Turgenev does not idealise them. They are also uncompromising, angular and capable of impulses of fierce indignation. But this does not make us love them less. On the contrary, the fact that they have weaknesses makes them more convincingly human. Further, their defects are those of their characteristic virtues. They have the angularity of a still untarnished youthful idealism: their fire burns with a beautiful white virginal flame. After all heroic virtue is uncompromising. And theirs is a heroic virtue, not the mere gentle sweetness of the typical "Good woman" of fiction. It is not that they are hard. Indeed, the sterner strain in them gives them an extraordinary pathos, mingled as it is with a spirit, tender, child-like and inexperienced, innocent of evil, vulnerable to suffering.

Turgenev's range is not confined to the beauty of virtue. He is also a master at conveying the complex charm of less reputable types of women: the brilliant, cold, honest Madame Odintsov of *Fathers and Children*, for example. Or Zinaida in *First Love*, passionate and ironical, melting and enigmatic. His portraits of the thoroughly bad reveals the same talent: Irina in *Smoke* is one of the few evil sirens of literature who convince us of their power to charm. The charm is not a wholly pleasing one; that is one of the most brilliant strokes in Turgenev's description. As the book proceeds and we get to know Irina better, she begins to jar on our moral taste just as she would have done in life. Her arts reveal themselves as contrived and meritricious; beside the pure true note sounded by the heroines, her personality rings false. Yet, her animal seductiveness, her subtle indolent accomplishment, are given their alluring force; so that we do not think it strange that the hero should have been subjugated by her. Well might a fine spirit succumb to something so dazzling and so civilised. Irina is an artist of the flesh; and an artist of a high order.

It is to Turgenev's female characters that we find ourselves recurring. This was natural, seeing that he was such an æsthete. The heroines are the objects of the hero's love. And love is the emotion most inextricably intertwined with the feeling for beauty; only when it is irradiated by the transfiguring light of love, is life to most people as beautiful as the artist longs for it to be. More than any other novelist, Turgenev describes it from the artist's point of view, discriminates with delicate accuracy the differing and characteristic æsthetic quality of its various moods and modes—rapture, jealousy, desire, romantic reverie—the boyish ardour of *First Love*, the mature man's sentiment that Lavretsky feels for Lisa, the throbbing, sensual obsession of *The Torrents of Spring*, the lyrical ideal passion of *On the Eve*. Yet, as always, Turgenev's preoccupation with æsthetic considerations never weakens his hold on

reality. His rendering of love is as true to sober experience as it is melodious.

Turgenev's æsthetic impulse is of the very substance
of his conceptions. It shows itself just as much, however,
in the form he imposes on his material. No one has ever
succeeded better in solving the central formal problem
which faces the novelist; to give a picture of life which
gives a convincing illusion of every-day reality but which
also has the shapeliness and continuous significance
that are the characteristic beauty of a work of art.
Turgenev's Russian sense of reality makes his illusion
perfect. Incident and character are photographically
true to objective fact; yet each has its part to play in
illustrating those underlying themes which give the
story significance. Lisa visits Lavretsky, who is falling
in love with her, at his country home. She is wearing a
straw hat with long ribbons. Turgenev does not imply
that there was anything unusual about it. No doubt
it was a pretty hat, but no masterpiece of the milliner's
art. Yet once we have read the story, we never forget
it. For to Lavretsky it seemed to incarnate that girlish
grace which draws him to Lisa so that the hat shines out
from the page, glorified by the glow of his dawning love.
Turgenev's special art shows itself first of all in his eye
for the significant detail and secondly in the self-
discipline which leads him to limit his account only to
those details that are significant. Nor does he make his
effects obvious by too much comment or explanation.
However complex the state of mind may be which he is
describing, he never analyses; but just picks out the
features in it that illustrate his point, and then leaves
the reader to draw his own conclusions.

The boyish hero of *First Love* passionately loves

K

Zinaida. From a fourteen-foot wall he watches her walking in the garden. She looks up at him, and says teasingly, "Jump down into the road to me, if you really do love me." Turgenev tells us nothing of the effect of her words on the boy's mind. He simply says that they acted on him literally like a push in the back: before he knows what he is doing he has made the fourteen-foot jump. No elaborate analysis could have conveyed so forcibly the obsessive, dominating quality of his passion. To take another instance from *Fathers and Children*. Madame Odintsov's feeling for Bazarov is extremely complex. He attracts her as no man has attracted her before. But the very strength of her sentiment rouses to combat it that strong self-protective spirit of independence which has up to then been the ruling force in her life. Torn between the two she knows not whether she loves him or not. Suddenly she gets a message to say that he is dying. She feels impelled to go to him at once; but, as she enters the sick-room and sees his altered deathly countenance, she is conscious only of a chill dismay; and the thought flashes through her, "If I had really loved him I should not have felt like this". One stroke: but no amount of explanation could have so vividly revealed her ultimate coldness; and also that honesty of mind which made her recognise it.

It is this economical certainty of touch which gives Turgenev's picture the continuous significance of art. His sense of shapeliness is equally sure. In an author so rigidly realistic this is even more remarkable. After all, life as we know it is the opposite of shapely; incorrigibly untidy, indeterminate, and heterogeneous. How is the artist, without distorting it, to compose it into a pleasing pattern? Indeed, few have done so more than once in their career. In England, Jane Austen; on the continent, Turgenev. His books do every justice to the claims of art. Every incident, every character contributes to the development of the central theme. Yet he never seems artful. The people have such independent reality, their relations to each other seem so much the spontaneous expression of their natures, that they appear to have organised themselves into a unity by happy chance, and just for the moment that we happen to be looking at them.

For the moment only. It is Turgenev's special achievement always to keep us aware of time and space beyond the story. The little group of people we see are part of the world outside which they have lived in before we meet them and to which they will return afterwards. The art by which he achieves this effect is as original as it is consummate. He has his own special formula which he uses again and again; but always with a new variation, so that no book is a repetition of another. Generally the scene is set in a country district where a group of people find themselves settled for a month or two. First Turgenev introduces us to them. As soon as they are clearly established in our imagination he goes back and gives us brief biographies; so we realise exactly who they are and what stage in their lives they have reached.

One of them—Rudin, Bazarov, Insarof, Lavretsky— is new to the others. His effect on the lives of the others is the theme of the story, the impact of his personality on them is the mainspring of the action. This action, often slight in itself, but deeply important, because of the issues it involves, occupies the main portion of the book. After it has drawn to its end, in a last short section, Turgenev briefly relates the subsequent fate of his characters, so that the ultimate consequence of the central action is disclosed for us. Thus, in a brief three hundred pages he is able to survey several lives, indicate their relation to the greater world outside and to those general laws of human fate of which even this greater world is but an illustration, while contriving to preserve the concentration, the lucid economical beauty of the highest classical art.

Indeed, Turgenev was rewarded for his undeviating devotion to æsthetic standards. He may not be the most powerful novelist, but who among the powerful novelists is so faultless a master of his craft? No one else of the same emotional scope has so satisfactorily solved the central problems that confront the writer of fiction. And the result has the serene special beauty of something done perfectly. In his pages we see life reflected as in the still waters of a lake, with every nuance of sky and cloud and pendant willow-tree reproduced with meticulous accuracy; and yet touched with an added enchantment that comes from the fact that they are mirrored in the transparent and gleaming element of Turgenev's art.

"ADOLPHE"

"ADOLPHE"

"ADOLPHE" has never been much read in England. It is too French. For all that the author happened to be a Swiss, his book is a typical French classic: and the French and English classic conceptions of fiction are poles apart. The English classical novelists, Fielding, Dickens and the rest of them, descend from Shakespeare. A novel to them, like a Shakespeare play, was first of all a vivid, varied entertainment, full of incident and strongly marked characters and humour and pathos and action. The French novel derives from a very different sort of drama, that of Racine; where we are presented with a single dramatic situation which is then logically developed to its conclusion. Its other parent is the French school of "moralist" writers, like Rochefoucauld and La Bruyère, who are concerned to analyse and define the springs of human conduct. The French classical novel, therefore, is out, not so much to entertain, as to illuminate. It is, first of all, a serious study of the principles governing human action. And its characteristics are logic, concentration, intellectual force. After the English novel it must seem, at first reading, a trifle bleak and monotone.

All this is intensely true of *Adolphe*. No great novel has a more limited canvas. This is deliberate. Benjamin Constant, its author, said that he wrote it partly to show that one could write a novel with only two characters, and involved all through in a single situation. It is a novel about an entanglement. Adolphe, a young man of twenty-three, ignorantly involves himself in a love affair with Ellénore, a woman two years older than himself, who, against her conscience, and forced largely by the pressure of unfortunate circumstances, has become the mistress of an older man for whom she doesn't feel deeply. Adolphe, though he has taken the initiative in the affair, soon discovers that he is not in love with her. She, on the other hand, becomes the victim of an obsessing passion for him. The story relates his struggles to get free from her. Fruitless struggles! Partly from guilt, partly from weakness, he never can, when it comes to the point, take that decisive action which will cut him free. Ellénore, though also haunted by guilt, clings blindly to the one thing which makes her life worth living, sacrificing more and more for him; and, by this means, making it harder and harder for him to break with her. Condemned to frustration and inaction, his life gradually grows empty and fruitless. At last Ellénore realises this; and the shock of realisation, combined with the anguish she feels at finding her love unrequited, kills her. But Adolphe's release comes too late. The long drawn-out struggle—it has lasted over six years—has sapped the power to act and believe within him. He is left an empty shell of a man, devoid alike of will or hope.

A story of inaction, not action; and it is told with an austere concentration. Not an episode, not a comment but refers to the main theme; no characters but the hero and heroine are described in more than bare outline; and even they are described almost exclusively in relation to the central situation. We are told far more about their intellectual and emotional make-up,

than about their appearance or demeanour or tricks
of speech. Indeed they do not speak much. Adolphe,
it is true, tells the story himself: but he doesn't reproduce
his conversations with others in dramatic form; he just
tells us the matter of what was said and the effect it had
on him, with a running analytic commentary. There is
a brief, brilliant account of his relations with his father—
his father is the only other sharply individualised
character in the story—but for the most part we see
Adolphe only in relation to himself and Ellénore, and
Ellénore only in relation to Adolphe. Further, the
drama has no background. The lovers move from
Germany to Bohemia, from Bohemia to Poland, but we
are shown nothing of these countries. Adolphe and
Ellénore are always, as it were, alone together in a
small, featureless sitting-room.

It is interesting that Constant should have limited
himself in this way; for there are signs that he could
describe background very well if he wanted. Almost at
the end of the story, when both the lovers have been
forced to realise the true position, and when Ellénore
is already sinking to death, they go for a short walk
with one another: and for once Constant does indicate
the landscape behind them. "It was," he says, "one of
those winter days when the sun shines sadly over the
greyish landscape as if it looked with pity on an earth
which it had ceased to warm. . . . The sky was serene,
the trees were leafless; not a breath stirred in the air, not
a bird crossed it: everything was motionless and the
only sound that made itself heard was that of the frozen
grasses as they broke beneath our feet." These brief
sentences show an acute sensibility to the physical scene,
a sharp perception of physical detail. Constant has

included them, however, not for their own sake but because they symbolise the mood of the hero and heroine. This mood is calm, there is even a tinge of tenderness in it. But it is a hopeless tenderness—like that of the sun shining without heat on the dead earth. Nowhere else in the story, we must suppose, did the author conceive the landscape background as being capable of thus enforcing the emotional significance of his drama. For nowhere else does he make use of his sense of landscape.

A similar deliberate severity shows itself in the style of the book. Just once or twice Constant allows himself an image: and then it is always extraordinarily brilliant and arresting. Ellénore, when Adolphe first meets her, fiery, sombre, fitful, troubled, makes an effect like that of a beautiful storm, "un bel orage"—the expression is almost untranslatable—Adolphe's last passages of untroubled love, faint reflections of the past, resemble "those pale faded leaves . . . that grow languidly on the branches of an uprooted tree". But for the most part the style is as plain and uncoloured as it can well be. Constant is deliberately out to create the illusion that he is not composing a literary work at all, but just giving us a bare exact record of fact.

Indeed, his is the most austere kind of art. This is appropriate to his subject. Frustration is a bleak distressing theme. And Constant puts in nothing to soften its painfulness. Nobody could read *Adolphe*, surely, to satisfy their wish-fulfilment dreams, or as a means of escape from the harsh facts of ordinary life. Always in it we are in the presence of reality, if not at its ugliest, yet at its saddest and most disillusioning. All the same, this monotonous, painful little tale of failure and futility is enthralling. Once one has read it one returns to it

again and again; and, always with growing admiration
and satisfaction. The satisfaction comes partly from
its formal perfection. As successfully as Jane Austen
and Turgenev, Constant solves the chief technical
problem facing the writer of fiction; he satisfies equally
the claims of life and art. Perhaps his achievement in
this respect is not quite so extraordinary as theirs, for he
does not try to impose unity on so diverse and complex
a scene. The French ideal of form did not let him.
Forced as he is to concentrate rigidly and exclusively
on his drama, he cannot make use of the material by
which Jane Austen and Turgenev suggest the presence
and movement of the rest of the world surrounding it,
which they contrive so wonderfully to incorporate into
their pattern. But, within its narrower scope, *Adolphe*
is just as realistically convincing as any of their books,
and just as shapely. As we have seen, every episode
furthers the action. For, in spite of its lack of incident,
there is an inner action. The book never stands still.
Each new phase in the story illustrates the growing
deterioration of the relation between hero and heroine:
and, as a consequence, of their characters under its
pressure. The end comes to us as inevitable as the final
chord of a Bach fugue. Yet though the book is so
logical, it never seems artificial. The development is so
true to experience as to seem quite free and spontaneous;
we seem to be watching something happening in real
life, not staged for us in the theatre of art.

This is partly due to the extraordinary convincingness
with which Constant sets his stage at the beginning.
Adolphe is introduced to us as exactly the sort of young
man who would be likely to get involved in such an
entanglement. By nature sensitive and romantic, he has

been brought up by a shy, formidable father, who hides
the fondness he feels for his son under a mask of ironical
detachment. The consequence has been that Adolphe
has grown up solitary, inhibited and—because he has
found that his naturally affectionate impulses met with
no response from the only person closely connected
with him—both emotionally unsatisfied and ignorant
about the processes of the heart. How natural then that
he should seek an outlet in love! How natural also, that,
misled by a gust of youthful passion, he should imagine
he was in love when in fact he was not! Ellénore is conceived with equal convincingness. She is not a light
woman; on the contrary, by temperament ardent, ex-
alted, and capable of a deep and faithful devotion, she is
miserable in the equivocal position in which unhappy circumstances have placed her. To be united for ever with
a man she admires and loves with her whole heart, like
Adolphe, becomes to her the one way by which she may
fulfil that better part of her nature, which has been up
to then wasted. With two such characters in such a
situation, a tragic development is inevitable. Both the
virtues and the vices of the actors combine to keep them
bound to one another. It is because Ellénore feels that
the finer part of her nature will find fulfilment in
Adolphe that she clings to him. All the same it is a
selfish clinging, and makes her unreasonable, predatory
and destructive. He, on the other hand, sticks to her
largely out of loyalty and pity. But also from weakness;
his unhappy childhood has engendered in him a
fundamental self-distrust which makes him incapable
of taking the responsibility of strong action, even when
his conscience tells him strong action is right. As a
result he too gets worse. The habit of weakness grows

on him, till in the end he has no will. There is a wonderful little stroke of human nature illustrating this at the
end of the story. On her death-bed Ellénore tells him
that she has left a letter written to him in a moment of
passionate resentment, which she wishes him to destroy
unread. He means to do so but when in fact he does
find it he can't help looking at the first few lines, and
then going on till he finishes it. Thus, in small things as
in great, his fatal weakness betrays itself.

The fluctuating phases of the intervening drama are
portrayed with an equal insight and subtlety: all its
complex movement of quarrel and reconciliation,
jealousy and remorse, false hope and final disillusionment. Listen to the account of the lovers' first quarrel.

"The scene became violent. We burst out in mutual
reproaches. Ellénore accused me of . . . having been
the cause that she was once more back again in that
equivocal situation in the eyes of other people, which
all her life she had been trying to get out of. I became
irritated to see her twisting into accusations against me,
the very things I had done because she wanted me to,
and for fear of distressing her. I complained of constraint, of my youth, wasted doing nothing, of the
tyranny she exercised over my smallest actions. While
I was saying all this, I noticed that she was in tears:
I stopped, I took back everything I had said, I poured
out explanations. We fell into each other's arms; but
the first blow had been struck, the first barrier passed.
We had both of us said irreparable things; and,
though we could be silent, we could not forget them."

Or this passage of analysis at a later stage in the

drama, where Ellénore has tried flirting with other
men as a means of reviving Adolphe's love.

"She thought of re-animating my love by rousing my
jealousy; this was only to stir ashes which nothing
could rekindle. Perhaps too, without realising it, a little
feminine vanity mingled with her calculation. She was
wounded by my coldness, so she wished to prove to
herself she still had the power of pleasing someone.
And, finally, perhaps in the loneliness of heart, where
I had left her, she found a kind of consolation in hearing
someone else repeat to her those words of love, which
from me she heard no longer."

How subtle this is, and how economical! A twisted,
complex knot of mixed motives disentangled in four
brief sentences. Most novelists would have taken ten
pages over it and then failed to make it clear. This
economy is an outstanding characteristic of Constant's
art. Again and again we come on a sentence which,
like a stone thrown into a pool, sets our thoughts
expanding in ever-growing circles of significance.
Listen to this:

"Man's sentiments are mixed and confused; they
are made up of a multitude of varied impressions which
escape exact observation; and words, always too crude
and too general, can serve to indicate but never to
define them."

Or

"Duplicity was foreign to my natural character;
but a man grows corrupt from the moment that he has

in his heart a single thought which he is constantly forced to dissimulate."

Or

"It's a big and irreparable step when one unveils suddenly before the eyes of a third person the hidden complexities of an intimate relationship; the daylight which penetrates into the sanctuary declares and completes that destruction, which has hitherto been hidden by the shades of night: as bodies shut up in tombs often keep their shape till the outer air is let in and reduces them to powder."

Such sentences set our reflections wandering far beyond the drama of Adolphe and Ellénore. Here we come to what sets *Adolphe* among the supreme masterpieces of fiction, to what makes it, not only a good, but a great book. It has a universal application. Constant has envisaged his story with such profound penetration that he reveals it as a particular instance of a universal law. Adolphe's tragedy is in a sense a particular one; it is largely due to that peculiar weakness of will, which is his characteristic sin. But as we contemplate it, the question strikes us, is this the fundamental cause? Is there not something fatal in the very nature of the passion in which he is involved? His history is only one instance of a situation which must always arise as long as the passion of love agitates the hearts of men and women; that false position which comes when two people, outwardly bound to each other, are inwardly at war; because one loves more than the other, and therefore demands something that the other cannot give. Some people may say that this is true of almost any

love affair.   Certainly a mutual passion of equal
strength is an ideal relation very seldom achieved in
this ill-proportioned world. But inequality of sentiment
does not generally lead to such catastrophic results
as in *Adolphe*. For one thing, few people are capable
of loving with the obsessing intensity of Ellénore.
For another, it is rare to get entangled deeply without feeling more for the other party than Adolphe
does. Rarely, in consequence, is the dilemma so acute:
or its results so fatal.   All the same, wherever there is
inequality of sentiment we are in the presence of what
is potentially, at least, "the Adolphe situation", with
all its accompanying emotional troubles; on the one
side jealousy and unsatisfied yearning, on the other,
constraint and frustration.   Everywhere there are
Ellénores and Adolphes to be found; and nowhere in
literature will they find their predicament portrayed
with so concentrated a truth as in the pages of Constant.
The tragedy of Adolphe's weakness is also the tragedy
of all unequal love.

But even when we have said this, we wonder if we
have said all. Is it not finally part of the inevitable
tragedy of human existence? If love is unsatisfying, is
not this because love is a manifestation of life? As
the drama mounts to its disastrous climax, and Adolphe
begins to review and look back on its long disillusioning course, he begins to see it in relation to his general
situation as a human being. In this new perspective,
it looks different. Why should he mind so much if his
life and talents are unfulfilled? What does fulfilment
mean? Helpless, ignorant and feeble, man is cast into
the world for a few brief years, to struggle as he can,
till death comes to cast him once more into darkness.

How insignificant our private, feverish little dramas seem in the shadow cast by the inescapable and terrible mystery of death. Death is, after all, the most important fact about life. Most intensely of all, this strikes Adolphe, as he watches Ellénore receive the last rites of the church on her death-bed.

"On my knees in the corner of her room at moments I lost myself in thought, at moments watched with an involuntary curiosity the other people gathered there —some frightened, some distracted—and also the singular power of custom to make people indifferent: so that the most solemn and terrifying ceremonies appear merely conventional and formal. I heard these men repeating the funeral words mechanically, just as if they also did not have to take part one day in a similar scene, just as if they also did not have to die one day. I was far from scorning these customs; is there a single one of them which ignorant man dares to call useless? They made Ellénore calm; they helped her to take this terrible step towards which we are all advancing without any of us being able to forsee what we shall then be feeling. I am not surprised that man needs a religion; what astonishes me is that he ever thinks himself strong enough and sufficiently safe from misfortune to dare repudiate one. He should, surely, in his weakness be led to invoke them all. In the thick darkness which surrounds us, is there a light we can reject? In the midst of the torrent which sweeps us away, is there a branch we dare refuse to hold on to?"

In this passage Adolphe's helplessness is revealed to us as only one example of that helplessness which is the

L

common characteristic of humanity; his predicament illustrates the universal predicament of mankind, as Constant conceived it. It is a peculiarly depressing conception, one must admit. For it stirs in us nothing of the sense of glory born in the midst of suffering, which we get from the more heroic types of tragedy. These mysteriously convince us that it is only in circumstances of extreme catastrophe that the human spirit rises to its full stature. Life at its most terrible turns out, paradoxically, to be also life at its most significant. There is nothing of this in *Adolphe*. Disaster does not intensify or exalt Adolphe's personality; it merely deflates it. His is a purely regrettable story of slow dreary defeat; and Constant compels us to savour every bitter drop of disillusionment and mortification which this defeat implies. However, this is not a fault. On the contrary, it is the ruthless though restrained consistency with which Constant is true to his grey vision that makes his achievement unique. Here, expressed once and for all—in faultless and imperishable form—is a picture of human existence, as seen by a spirit, honest, intelligent, sensitive; but without faith, without hope.

TWO TWENTIETH-CENTURY NOVELISTS:

1. VIRGINIA WOOLF

2. E. M. FORSTER

VIRGINIA WOOLF AND E. M. FORSTER

THE critic may well hesitate before passing judgment on an author less than thirty years older than himself. Consider the shocking blunders committed by those who have tried to do it. Matthew Arnold thought poorly of Tennyson; Saint-Beuve spoke in slighting terms of Flaubert; Dr. Johnson said that the taste for Sterne was a fashion that would soon pass. That such distinguished persons should err thus flagrantly is more startling than surprising. Judging contemporary or near-contemporary literature is a task of peculiar difficulty. For one thing, every original writer is likely to be an innovator either in form or matter. Anyone coming fresh to his work must find it hard to see his innovations in the right focus. If he likes them, he is liable to think them more epoch-making than in fact they are. If—and this is more probable—they bewilder him, he is tempted to dismiss them as perverse and pretentious nonsense. Again, a vital writer generally represents a strongly defined and controversial attitude to the life and thought of his time. The critic represents one too. How then can he help being biased for or against his subject, according as how far he sympathises with him? It must have been almost impossible forty years ago for an anti-imperialist to be fair to Kipling, to approach him in that detached yet receptive frame of mind necessary to appreciate him justly. He feared Kipling's influence too much.

Whereas he could easily swallow Shakespeare's jingo patriotism; Shakespeare lived too long ago, and in too different a world, for his influence to be dangerous. Finally—and here he is faced with a more subtle obstacle to accurate judgment—the contemporary critic finds it hard to distinguish what is permanent in an author's work from what is ephemeral. Only that part will be permanent which expresses the author's individual first-hand vision of experience. Much would-be creative writing does not do this, but only reflects conceptions of life current in his time. Scott's heroes for instance are merely pictures of the ideal gentleman as conceived in his day: his peasants on the other hand are drawn straight from life. In his time readers did not feel the difference very acutely, for the heroes were for them animated by the vitality of the ideal which they represented. Now, when that ideal no longer prevails, we recognise them to be shadows; whereas the peasants are still breathing flesh-and-blood.

In view of all these difficulties, it might appear that critics would be wiser not to write about their contemporaries at all. This however is not so. For though their vision will almost certainly be a trifle distorted, yet it should also in some respects penetrate deeper than that of a subsequent critic ever can. The contemporary critic is in the position of a man writing a book about his father. Clearly he cannot expect to be unbiased about him, nor to see him in true perspective with the rest of mankind. On the other hand he is bound to know him much more intimately than any outsider will do. So with the critic. To be impartial about a contemporary writer will be impossible to him,

or to assess his position finally in the hierarchy of
English letters. But, living in the same world as he is,
he will better understand his terms of reference and
should be able to enter more closely into his feelings.
He has got something to tell his readers that no critic
of a later generation can know. But before he begins his
task he must approach his subject in a different spirit
to that in which he would treat a writer of the past.
He must recognise that there is simply no question of
his coming to a final judgment. He is merely recording
a personal impression, incomplete, provisional, ex-
ploratory, and which he realises will certainly be
modified by posterity.

Such are the considerations that must occur to anyone who, at this moment of time, aspires to make an
estimate of Virginia Woolf and E. M. Forster. The
critic can be sure of one thing only—both are genuine
creative artists; novelists, that is, whose works are
valuable not primarily for the ideas they contain or the
information they give us, but because they do introduce
us to a unique and living imaginative world. Unique
but also akin: Forster and Virginia Woolf have
enough in common to be considered together. Both
are highly civilised persons in whom an exquisite
sensibility and an acute, inquisitive intelligence have
been developed to the finest point of fastidious refinement. Developed, too, under the influence of the same
culture, that English brand of liberal culture which
grew up in the later part of the nineteenth century.
Its outstanding characteristic is a blend of intellectual
freedom with material security. It was certainly very
secure, sheltered even: the product of an England
strong, prosperous, humane, progressing every year on

the road of civilisation, protected apparently from any threat of a relapse into barbarism. Our two writers, moreover, came from the most sheltered part of it. Comfortable if not rich, they were the children of the middle class: neither expected to take part in the harsh responsibilities of government on the one hand, nor forced into the struggle for existence on the other. Temperamentally, too, they were likely to be strongly influenced by the sheltered quality of their surroundings. For their natural bias was for the private, the personal; books, friendship, meditation appealed to them far more than action, especially action on the broad public stage. Both react violently against the pressure of the crowd; neither is at home in the presence of large public problems. Mr. Forster indeed is aware of them: at times he even feels obliged by his conscience to have views about them; about the Indian question and the public school question and the class question. But it is characteristic that these views are always conceived in personal and individual terms. He judges public issues by the standards of private life. As for Virginia Woolf, in her fiction at any rate, she just splendidly ignores them.

But if materially sheltered, these two writers are as free mentally as human beings can ever have been. The liberal tradition is protestant, individualist, nonconformist, questioning, regarding it as the first duty of man to be true to his own personal sense of what is right. And Mr. Forster and Virginia Woolf—coming as they do at the end of its development—carry these principles to their extreme conclusion. They suspect authority, tradition, convention, wherever they find them: in thought, in religion in the social system.

Each is engaged in discovering his or her view of life bit by bit and without regard to the pressure of any sort of public opinion; and then, equally boldly, in creating a literary vehicle in which to incarnate it.

1

VIRGINIA WOOLF

This common belief in the individual approach makes them soon diverge from one another. Virginia Woolf was the more experimental of the two. Like all serious novelists she was out to point a true picture of life as she saw it, and she very soon came to the conclusion that any of the systems by which other people had attempted to impose an order on experience did not seem to her to correspond with reality. It was not just a question of breaking with the past—she was as little satisfied with the rationalist and materialist order of Wells and Arnold Bennett as she was with the ideal and religious patterns accepted by older writers. "Look within," she says, "and life, it seems, is very far from being 'like this'. Examine for a moment an ordinary mind on an ordinary day. The mind receives a myriad impressions—trivial, fantastic, evanescent, or engraved with the sharpness of steel. From all sides they come, an incessant shower of innumerable atoms; and as they fall, as they shape themselves into the life of Monday or Tuesday, the accent falls differently from of old; the moment of importance came not here but there; so that, if a writer were a free man and not a slave, if he could write what he chose, not what he must, if he could base his work upon his own feeling and not upon convention, there would be no plot, no comedy, no tragedy, no love interest or catastrophe in the accepted style, and perhaps not a single button sewn on as the Bond Street tailors would have. Life is not a series of gig lamps symmetrically arranged; life is a luminous halo, a semi-transparent envelope surrounding us from the beginning of consciousness to the end. Is it not the task of the novelist to convey this varying, this unknown and uncircumscribed spirit, whatever aberration or complexity it may display, with as little mixture of the alien and external as possible?" So she conceived her task, so she tried to execute it. The luminous halo, the semi-transparent envelope is her subject. Through the eyes of one or more of her characters she strove simply to record the actual process of living, to trace the confused succession of impression and thought and mood, as it drifted cloud-like across the clear mirror of consciousness.

It might have been expected that the resulting effect would be merely chaotic. So it would have been had she in fact rigidly followed her theory. Luckily, she did not. She has cast away other people's gig lamps, but she can't help lighting some new ones of her own. Instinctively she picks out for emphasis only those features of her subject which strike her as peculiarly significant. So that all the disordered matter of experience falls into a pattern imposed by the predominant motive force in her own inner life. This was her sensibility to the beautiful. Virginia Woolf was in the fullest, highest, extremest sense of the word, an æsthete. The most significant moments in her life were its moments of intense æsthetic experience. As much as Keats she loved "the principle of beauty in all things": and she makes it her first aim to discover it. Martin in her book, on the way to Mrs. Dalloway's

party, might be a symbol for his creator on her journey
through human life.

"Here he was starting to go to a party, at his age,
with the belief upon him that he was about to have an
experience. But what?

Beauty anyhow. Not the crude beauty of the eye.
It was not beauty pure and simple—Bedford Place
leading into Russell Square. It was straightness and
emptiness of course; the symmetry of a corridor; but
it was also windows lit up, a piano, a gramophone
sounding; a sense of pleasure-making hidden, but now
and again emerging when, through the uncurtained
window, the window left open, one saw parties sitting
over tables, young people slowly circling, conversations
between men and women, maids idly looking out (a
strange comment, theirs, when work was done),
stockings drying on top ledges, a parrot, a few plants.
Absorbing, mysterious, of infinite richness, this life."

Virginia Woolf's picture of the world, then is primarily a picture of those aspects of it that stir her
imagination and sense of beauty. The ugly and
æsthetically insignificant she passes by; or admits only
as they may serve as foil to the beauty that precedes and
follows them. Thus she creates her perspective: thus
she designs per pattern.

This concentration on the æsthetic aspects of life
gives her picture other characteristics. Æsthetic
experiences are contemplative affairs. So also are the
big moments in Virginia Woolf's books. Action, event,
play hardly any part in them at all. The sight of a
London park in Autumn may fill the foreground of her

canvas: the fact that there is a European war on at the same moment is a mere insignificant incident in the background. She will take a chapter to describe a casual stroll in which a woman feels quickened to a deeper apprehension of experience: her death or marriage Virginia Woolf may pass over in a parenthesis. Indeed the title of her last book *Between the Acts* indicates her feeling that active drama supplies only a superficial view of life. The things that really matter happen "between the acts".

Contemplation is a lonely affair. Here we come to a second consequence of the æsthetic approach. Virginia Woolf's characters are presented to us essentially as solitaries. Their inner life is what really matters about them. Even in company, they seem to be alone, absorbed in private unspoken trains of thought. Their relations to others are only valuable to them in so far as they feed and enrich their solitary experience, as they contribute to their moments of inner illumination and ecstasy. Not that their creator is only concerned to record moments of ecstasy. Her picture of life is far from being a consistently bright one. It has a sadness inseparable from its joy. When æsthetic receptiveness flags, when the imagination ceases to respond to the spectacle of the world, a terrifying sense of universal emptiness, a chill, as of spiritual death, assaults the spirit. Some of Virginia Woolf's most memorable passages are concerned with describing this phenomenon. Listen to Bernard in *The Waves*.

"This self now as I leant over the gate looking down over fields rolling in waves of colour beneath me made no answer. He threw up no opposition. He attempted no phrase. His fist did not form. I waited. I listened. Nothing came, nothing. I cried then with a sudden conviction of complete desertion. Now there is nothing. No fin breaks the waste of this immeasurable sea. Life has destroyed me. No echo comes when I speak, no varied words. This is more truly death than the death of friends, than the death of youth. I am the swathed figure in the hairdresser's shop taking up only so much space. ... The woods had vanished; the earth was a waste of shadow. No sound broke the silence of the wintry landscape. No cock crowed; no smoke rose; no train moved. A man without a self, I said. A heavy body leaning on a gate. A dead man. With dispassionate despair, with entire disillusionment, I surveyed the dust dance; my life, my friends' lives, and those fabulous presences, men with brooms, women writing, the willow tree by the river—clouds and phantoms made of dust too, of dust that changed, as clouds lose and gain and take gold or red and lose their summits and billow this way and that, mutable, vain. I, carrying a notebook, making phrases, had recorded merely changes; a shadow, I had been sedulous to take note of shadows. How can I proceed now, I said, without a self, weightless and visionless, through a world weightless, without illusion?"

Further, Virginia Woolf's delight in beauty brings a correspondingly acute awareness of its frailty. Indeed, if her first impulse is to express life's loveliness, her second is to express its transience; life drifts past her like a cloud, shifting, changing, dissolving, even as she gazes. The fact of its fleetingness creates a sadness and bewilderment, a sense of unresolved discord at the very heart of her vision of experience. What is one to make of an existence in which what appears supremely significant and valuable is at the same time so ephemeral? Once more like Keats, she is oppressed by the melancholy that lives with "Beauty that must die, and joy whose hand is ever at his lips, bidding adieu." The fact of beauty on the one hand, the fact of mutability on the other, these are the two poles on which her panorama of human experience revolves.

In her earlier novels she is content merely to display it without offering any explanation. Life, as shown in *Jacob's Room* and *Mrs. Dalloway*, is an insoluble mystery. But Virginia Woolf was too searching and too profound a spirit not to try and pierce deeper; and in her later works she seems to be feeling after some explanation for the enigma. There are hints that at moments she has attained to a vision of some ultimate principle of beauty, outside the flux of mortal things. The artist characters in these works—and an æsthete like her turns first to the artist as the person most likely to throw light on the riddle of the universe—have glimpses of it. In the last paragraph of *To the Lighthouse* Lily Bristow finishes the picture on which she has been at work throughout the story. Up till then she has always felt frustrated by an inability to devise some centre to her design which should draw it into a unity.

"Quickly, as if she were recalled by something over there, she turned to her canvas. There it was—her picture. Yes, with all its green and blues, its lines running up and across, its attempt at something. It would be hung in the attics, she thought; it would be destroyed. But what did that matter, she asked herself, taking up her brush again. She looked at the steps; they were empty; she looked at her canvas; it was blurred. With a sudden intensity, as if she saw it clear for a second, she drew a line there, in the centre. It was done; it was finished. Yes, she thought, laying down her brush in extreme fatigue, I have had my vision."

And the vision of the picture stands symbol for Lily's whole vision of human experience. At the culminating moment of successful creation the artist sees the fragmentary multi-coloured confusion of life revealed as the expression of an underlying spiritual order. At the end of *The Years* Virginia Woolf carried her conjectures a step further; in veiled, tentative fashion she suggests that there is a strain in the human spirit which is part of eternal reality, and which is inevitably unsatisfied as long as it is imprisoned in the wearisome condition of mortality: but which may, after it is freed from it, at last find fulfilment. Eleanor, at seventy years old, looks back on a life, whose significance eludes her.

"There must be another life, she thought, sinking back into her chair, exasperated. Not in dreams; but here and now, in this room, with living people. She felt as if she were standing on the edge of a precipice with her hair blown back; she was about to grasp something that just evaded her. There must be another life, here and now, she repeated. This is too short, too broken. We know nothing, even about ourselves. We're only just beginning, she thought, to understand, here and there. She hollowed her hands in her lap, just as Rose had hollowed hers around her ears. She held her hands hollowed; she felt that she wanted to enclose the present moment; to make it stay; to fill it fuller and fuller, with the past, the present and the future, until it shone, whole, bright, deep with understanding. . . . It's useless, she thought, opening her hands. It must drop. It must fall. And then? she thought; for her too there would be the endless night; the endless dark. She looked ahead of her as though she saw opening in front of her a very long dark tunnel. But, thinking of the dark, something baffled her; in fact it was growing light."

The end of life, so Virginia Woolf ponders, may be no blank, dark wall, but rather an opening into a region of .light, where all is at last made clear. In *Between the Acts* she seems to be yet another step ahead nearer penetrating the mystery. After the successful performance of her pageant a wave of depression overwhelms its authoress, Miss La Trobe, as she realises how ephemeral her work is. She may have achieved her aim but like everything else in life, achievement passes. Then her mood changes; she forgets to be melancholy as the idea of her next work begins to shape itself in her mind. But can this mean— so Virginia Woolf seems to be asking herself—that the discord in the heart of things is not after all unresolvable; that so far from the mutable being inevitably at odds with the eternal, it is, on the contrary, its image and temporal incarnation. Perhaps in the very unceasing process of death and renewal the timeless principle of beauty manifests itself to men. The thought is something like that which stole into Wordsworth's

M

mind as he gazed at the ever-flowing waters of the River Duddon.

> "For backward Duddon as I cast my eyes
> I see what was and is and will abide;
> Still glides the stream, and shall for ever glide;
> The form remains, the function never dies."

However these hints and glimpses are only hints and glimpses. They do not amount to a firm, clear faith. Rare and vague, they fail to dissipate the general impression of doubtful mystery—life floating by in its mingling of beauty and sadness, as elusive and insubstantial as a shred of mist—which permeates the books, and the vision of which is their subject.

It is very unlike the vision presented by other novelists; and excludes some of the chief sources of their effects. There is no room for drama in it. Drama depends on the clash of character: and how can people clash with one another if each is enclosed in an envelope—even though it be a semi-transparent one? Imprisoned as they are, each in the solitary confinement of his own consciousness, the characters in Virginia Woolf's books never come into direct contact. Indeed, character, in the objective sense, hardly exists for her. Seen through the shifting haze of the observer's mood other people's individualities lose their clear-cut outline; while the observer's own self is dissolved into a succession of impressions.

Virginia Woolf's exclusive concentration on the æsthetic aspects of experience also prevents her from envisaging its moral aspects. People in her books are shown as happy and sad, beautiful and ugly but seldom as bad and good. Nor, in any consistent way, as loving

or hating; the climate in which they live is cold and
ethereal, the heart does not grow warm there for love
or hate. How curiously detached and distant do the
children in her books—Elizabeth Dalloway, Cam
and James Ramsay—seem from their parents, in spite
of an occasional impulse of affection or exasperation.
Even when Virginia Woolf describes a happy marriage
like that of Mr. and Mrs. Ramsay in *To the Lighthouse*,
she gets no further than indicating that at brief moments
they felt an unusual harmony of soul one with the
other. "We perish each alone," murmurs Mr. Ramsay
to himself as he paces the beach. All Virginia Woolf's
characters might have said the same thing. Not that
she seems to regret it. On the contrary, as we have
seen, solitude is for her the condition of the richest
experience of which the human spirit is capable. And
she looks on any attempt to violate the privacy of that
solitude as the greatest menace that can threaten the
soul. Stephen in *Mrs. Dalloway*, Rhoda in *The Waves*,
commit suicide simply because they feel they cannot
otherwise escape such a violation, and in a strange and
significant passage of *Mrs. Dalloway* the heroine bursts
out in shuddering diatribe against love and religion,
two forces which, so she suspects, are always trying to
break down those barriers necessary to preserve what
to her is spiritually most precious in life.

"The cruellest things in the world, she thought,
seeing them clumsy, hot, domineering, hypocritical,
eavesdropping, jealous, infinitely cruel and unscrupulous, dressed in a mackintosh coat, on the landing;
love and religion. Had she ever tried to convert
anyone herself? Did she not wish everybody merely to

be themselves? And she watched out of the window the old lady opposite climbing upstairs. Let her climb upstairs if she wanted to; let her stop; then let her, as Clarissa had often seen her, gain her bedroom, part her curtains, and disappear again into the background. Somehow one respected that—that old woman looking out of the window, quite unconscious that she was being watched. There was something solemn in it—but love and religion would destroy that, whatever it was, the privacy of the soul."

A novel without drama, without moral values, and without character or strong personal emotion—it is a hard thing to write: and it cannot be said that Virginia Woolf is always successful. Sometimes she fails because she goes outside our own self-appointed limitations, because her plot entails her presenting aspects of life which her vision inevitably excludes. *Night and Day*, her second novel, errs in this respect. It is a love story in which each lover appears so solitary and self-absorbed as to make it impossible for the reader to believe in his or her passion. For similar reasons in *Mrs. Dalloway* Virginia Woolf fails to convince us of the reality of Rezia's grief when her husband kills himself. At other times she attempts, unsuccessfully, to draw characters in the objective external convention of the traditional novel. Hugh Whitbread and Sir William Bradshaw are carefully observed portraits; but because their creator does not draw them from the inside they never come to life. They are meticulously dressed dummies, mere conventional types of snobbish worldling and hard, power-loving careerist. Moreover they are drawn in a spirit of moral indignation. This puts them out of focus with the rest of Virginia Woolf's picture. What basis is there for moral indignation in a world not concerned with moral values? Their only effect is to make us feel that Virginia Woolf has forgotten her art in a capricious outburst of temper against two types of person whom she has chanced in life to find irritating.

Elsewhere she errs in the other direction. Her picture is so concerned with the inner life as to destroy our sense of the reality of the outer. This surely stops her most ambitious venture, *The Waves*, from making the impression at which it aims. The five characters who in successive monologue present us with their vision of experience are never distinguished sufficiently from each other to acquire individuality. Wrapt in the luminous halo of which she speaks, their characteristic outlines grow fogged and blurred. Indeed the balance between the internal world, which is her subject, and the external, to which she must convince us that it is in fact related, is extremely delicate. Only in *To the Lighthouse* does she succeed in preserving it throughout a whole book. Elsewhere, like so many English novelists, Virginia Woolf impresses by the heights to which she rises, rather than by the level of perfection she maintains.

But what heights they are! As might be expected, they are heights of beauty, they reveal her æsthetic sensibility. This is not of an abnormal sort; if it was, it would not have such force. Virginia Woolf reacts spontaneously and healthily to those things that mankind has always thought beautiful: to sunsets and fair faces, to crocuses and diamond necklaces and St. Paul's Cathedral. But how much more rich than the ordinary man's is her appreciation of them, and how much more discriminating! Exactly she isolates the precise quality in each which gives it its charm; and she suggests also the imaginative perfume which breathes from it, the train of exquisite associations that it evokes. Here is a landscape:

"The houses falling away on both sides, they came out on the quay, and the whole bay spread before them and Mrs. Ramsay could not help exclaiming, 'Oh, how beautiful!' For the great plateful of blue water was before her; the hoary lighthouse, distant, austere, in the midst; and on the right, as far as the eye could see, fading and falling, in soft low pleats, the green sand dunes with the wild flowing grasses on them, which always seemed to be running away into some moon country, uninhabited of men."

Equally precisely she can convey the æsthetic flavour of the world of man. It may be a Georgian country house, abounding in the sense of its period:

"She waited for a moment in the hall. Her eyes were dimmed after the glare of the road. Everything seemed pale and frail and friendly. The rugs were faded; the pictures were faded. Even the Admiral in his cocked hat over the fireplace wore a curious look of faded urbanity. In Greece one was always going back two thousand years. Here it was always the eighteenth century. Like everything English, she thought, laying down her umbrella on the refectory table beside the china bowl, with dried rose leaves in it, the past seemed near, domestic, friendly."

But Virginia Woolf's æsthetic response is not confined to the accepted, recognised and official objects of beauty. Not only does she illuminate our appreciation of what we already think beautiful, she opens our eyes to new sources of delight. Far more successfully than any contemporary poet has she disengaged the æsthetic quality in the modern scene. In the first chapter of *Mrs. Dalloway* a summer morning in Bond Street, all buses and policemen and clamouring shoppers, is made to glow with the splendour of a picture by Vermeer. How pictorial is King's Cross Station, how poetical a stream-lined railway engine, as seen by Lady Lasswade arriving to take the night train for the north.

"Just in time, she said to herself. The usual exhilaration mounted in her as she walked along the platform. Diffused light poured down from a great height. Men's cries and the clangour of shunting carriages echoed in the immense vacancy. The train was waiting; travellers were making ready to start. Some were standing with one foot on the step of the carriage drinking out of thick cups as if they were afraid to go far from their seats. She looked down the length of the train and saw the engines sucking water from a hose. It seemed all body, all muscle; even the neck had been consumed into the smooth barrel of the body. This was 'The' train; the others were toys in comparison. She snuffed up the sulphurous air, which left a slight tinge of acid at the back of the throat, as if it already had a tang of the north."

These pictures are so fully visualised as to seem the work of a painter rather than a writer. A realistic painter too: here we come to the second outstanding

quality in her sensibility. Most writers specialise
in the beautiful spill of golden glaze of romantic sentiment over their subject, softening its harsher aspects.
Not so Virginia Woolf. "How exactly Bond Street!"
we exclaim. "How exactly like a railway engine. But I
never knew it was so lovely." For always she combines
beauty with accuracy, and gets her effect, not by
idealising and decorating it, but simply by isolating and
indicating those aspects of her subject that appeal to
the æsthetic sense. She mentions the red hands of the
saleswoman in a Bond Street flower shop, but in order
to add a ravishing note of colour to her composition.

"Mrs. Dalloway advanced, light, tall, very upright,
to be greeted at once by button-faced Miss Pym, whose
hands were always bright red, as if they had been stood
in cold water with the flowers. There were flowers:
delphiniums, sweet peas, bunches of lilac; and carnations, masses of carnations. There were roses; there
were irises. Ah, yes—so she breathed in the earthy
garden sweet smell."

This account of Miss Pym has a glint of humour.
Here we come to another distinguishing strain in
Virginia Woolf's feeling for the beautiful. It is not
solemn. Most professional exponents of the beautiful
write mainly in a mood of ecstatic elevation or delicate
gravity; and about subjects appropriate to such a state
of feeling. Their most characteristic passages are
poetical rhapsodies. Virginia Woolf can write such
passages with the best of them.

"But what after all is one night? A short space,

especially when the darkness dims so soon, and so soon
a bird sings, a cock crows, or a faint green quickens,
like a turning leaf, in the hollow of the wave. Night,
however, succeeds to night. The winter holds a pack
of them in store and deals them equally, evenly, with
indefatigable fingers. They lengthen; they darken.
Some of them hold aloft clear planets, plates of
brightness. The autumn trees, ravaged as they are,
take on the flash of tattered flags kindling in the gloom
of cool cathedral caves where gold letters on marble
pages describe death in battle and how bones bleach
and burn far away in Indian sands. The autumn trees
gleam in the yellow moonlight, in the light of harvest
moons, the light which mellows the energy of labour,
and smooths the stubble, and brings the wave lapping
blue to the shore."

Ruskin himself never soared more lyrically than this.
But Virginia Woolf's sensibility exhibits itself just as
brilliantly in a playful mood, and in response to objects
generally thought of as frivolous; about a balldress
just as much as about the autumn moonlight.

"Nancy, dressed at enormous expense by the greatest
artists in Paris, stood there looking as if her body had
merely put forth, of its own accord, a green frill."

In *A Room of One's Own* Virginia Woolf even describes
a well-cooked luncheon in such a way as to make it a
thing of beauty and a joy for ever.

"The lunch on this occasion began with soles, sunk in
a deep dish, over which the College cook had spread a

counterpane of the whitest cream, save that it was branded here and there with brown spots as on the flanks of a doe. After this came the partridges, but if this suggests a couple of bald brown birds on a plate you are mistaken. The partridges, many and various, came with all their retinue of sauces and salads, the sharp and the sweet, each in its order; then potatoes, thin as coins but not so hard; then sprouts foliated as roses but more succulent. And no sooner had the roast and its retinue been done with, than the silent serving man . . . set before us, wreathed in napkins, a confection which rose all sugar from the waves. To call it pudding and relate it to rice and tapioca would be an insult."

This lighter, more humorous strain in such a passage is an expression of yet another quality: her intelligence. The sense of beauty does not lull her into an unthinking, rapturous dream. Her vision—and this serves still further to save it from romantic unreality—quivers with the incessant activity of her acute and ironical observation. However enchanted she may be, she is always able to notice and to smile. Sensibility and intelligence mingle together in a clear stream which ripples over the objects of her contemplation making them gleam out with an extraordinary brilliance and distinctness. Indeed she is as acute as she is sensitive. With what an extraordinary subtlety and truth does she observe the course of that inner process of thought and feeling which is her subject! To take only a single illustration:

" 'Yes, take it away,' Mrs. Ramsay said briefly, interrupting what she was saying to Mr. Bankes to speak to the maid. 'It must have been fifteen—no, twenty years ago—that I last saw her,' she was saying, turning back to him again as if she could not lose a moment of their talk, for she was absorbed by what they were saying. So he had actually heard from her this evening! And was Carrie still living at Marlow, and was everything still the same? Oh, she could remember it as if it were yesterday—going on the river, feeling very cold. But if the Mannings made a plan they stuck to it. Never should she forget Herbert killing a wasp with a teaspoon on the bank! And it was still going on, Mrs. Ramsay mused, gliding like a ghost among the chairs and tables of that drawing-room on the banks of the Thames where she had been so very, very cold twenty years ago; and it fascinated her, as if, while she had changed, that particular day, now become very still and beautiful, had remained there, all these years. Had Carrie written to him herself? she asked.

"'Yes. She says they're building a new billiard room', he said. No! No! That was out of the question! Building a billiard room! It seemed to her impossible.

"Mr. Bankes could not see that there was anything very odd about it. They were very well off now. Should he give her love to Carrie?

"'Oh', said Mrs. Ramsay with a little start, 'No', she added, reflecting that she did not know this Carrie who built a new billiard room. But how strange, she repeated, to Mr. Bankes' amusement, that they should be going on still. For it was extraordinary to think that they had been capable of going on living all these years when she had not thought of them more than once all that time. How eventful her own life had been, during those same years. Yet perhaps Carrie Manning had not thought about her either. The thought was strange and distasteful."

How brilliant this is and how convincing! For it is in casual and apparently trivial symbols like that of the billiard room, that we recall and visualise other people; and draw our sad conclusions on time and change, and friendship dissolving under their involuntary, irresistible pressure. By a snatch of talk it is suddenly brought home to us how far we have drifted from those Carries who once we knew so well, but who now, uncharacteristically, are building themselves new billiard rooms. So, now shadowed, now sparkling, now swift, now slow, its surface variegated by countless checks and eddies and leaps and gushes and with all manner of irrelevant little leaves and twigs wafted on to it, of associations past and present, does the stream of our minute-to-minute thought and feeling flow continuously by.

Yet Virginia Woolf never forgets to describe it as an artist, and not as a mere unselective photographer. Passed through the filter of her fastidious taste, the current of consciousness is cleared of those lumps of tedium or squalor which make it, when portrayed by other hands, so incurably unappetising a spectacle. Virginia Woolf's close realistic observation of the human mind is always kept harmonious with her æsthetic vision of life. Indeed it enhances its effect. Not only as we have seen does it anchor it to the earth, prevent it becoming too dreamy and ethereal; it also keeps it interesting. Pure beauty, page after page of it, is, we must face the fact, a little dull. One cannot read descriptions indefinitely. Moreover, Virginia Woolf is trying to create a world of human beings, not

of inanimate objects, and human beings, if we are to
believe in their existence, must be endowed with more
features than a pair of eyes. Virginia Woolf's picture
of life as a thing of beauty is enlivened all the time by
little strokes of humour and observation; it is diversified
by an incessantly changing procession of moods; it is
made vital by her unsleeping curiosity about everything
great and small that comes within her line of vision.

She is by far the most satisfying of æsthetes. She is
not the first. It is even possible that literary historians
of the future will see her primarily as the culmination
of the nineties, and that movement of which Walter
Pater was the high priest in England. Certainly there
is a great deal in common between him and her.
Like her, Pater regarded life as a succession of contemplative moments to be filled with as rich a content
as possible; like her he directed our eyes to look first
and everywhere for what stimulates the sense of beauty.
But Pater practised less well than he preached.
Whatever his principles may have been, in fact he
looked for æsthetic satisfaction only in a very limited
area of experience: the beautiful for him was mostly to
be found in museums. Not so Virginia Woolf. She
could find it as much in a scrap of orange peel lying
in the gutter as in the Venus de Milo, as easily walking
down the Euston Road as within the consecrated portals
of the National Gallery. There is nothing languid or
academic about her æstheticism. Casual and zestful,
it is the expression of an intense vitality, at home in the
bustle and clamour of the modern age, inspired by no
fatigued desire to escape from a present that is too
much for her into the safe calm of a dead past. As
presented by her, the æsthetic life is as vigorous and

satisfying as any other kind of life. And for us too, while we are reading her books: as long as their spell is on us we do not bother about the limitations of her vision. Indeed these limitations are seen to be a necessary condition of her success. In order to concentrate our eyes on the æsthetic aspects of experience, she has to exclude its other aspects. And they seem more beautiful for being thus isolated. Her coldness, her detachment from the hot earth, add to her vision a sea-fresh purity, a pearly gleam which set the spirit astir with a sort of delicate exhilaration. What a relief for once in a way, freed from the claims of heart and conscience, to concentrate on the mere spectacle of a world so brimful of strangeness and fascination and delight! How cleansing to be transported, if only for an hour, to a region where it is more important to be clever than to be good, and more important to be beautiful than to be either!

2

E. M. FORSTER

Mr. E. M. Forster is not a revolutionary author in the sense that Virginia Woolf was. Indeed, to turn from one of her books to his is to feel oneself transported back almost into the age of Meredith and Henry James. For here once more is a regular plot, here are characters, conversations, comic relief; here also are moral judgments. These above all. Mr. Forster is as much a didactic writer as George Eliot herself. Though pulsing with intelligence and sensibility, he does not make these his ultimate standard of value, or look on them as the most important things in life. When he sets out to draw the world, it is its moral aspects that strike him most forcibly. The categories in which he ranges people are primarily moral, the pattern he imposes on experience is the pattern of his moral vision.

Here it is, though, that his originality shows itself. Mr. Forster's moral vision is a fresh, private, independent affair, owing something no doubt to previous moral systems, but not the same as any of them. To see human nature from his point of view is to see it in a new moral perspective. This point of view owes its individuality to the fact that Mr. Forster unites in himself two qualities seldom found together. He is at once tender-hearted and unattached. Unattached congenitally:

he feels himself part of no corporate unit, seems temperamentally unresponsive to those instinctive, irrational, magnetic forces that draw the individual into a group; national feeling, class feeling, family feeling, comradely feeling. Even the more primitive animal emotions, which link people otherwise diverse, do not mean much to him, if we are to judge by his account of them. Sex in his stories is a curiously bloodless and uncompelling affair. The only emotional relation between human beings into which he enters fully is friendship, that exquisite sense of a mutual sympathy of heart and mind which occasionally arises between independent individuals. The very sensitiveness which makes such friendship delightful also makes it precarious. Any jarring note—an error of taste, a failure of sympathy—can destroy it completely. Mr. Forster notices this and draws his conclusions. The differences between human beings strike him far more forcibly than the characteristics that they have in common.

They strike him unpleasantly, however. Here is where his tender-heartedness comes in. Affectionate, dependent, yearning to love and to be loved, the personality that declares itself through his books holds that only in close relation to another person can the finest part of a man's nature find fulfilment. Mr. Forster is the opposite of the Miller of Dee in the old song, who sang so jollily, because he cared for no one and nobody cared for him. Not for Mr. Forster the satisfactions of Virginia Woolf's æsthetic solitude; self-sufficient intellectual persons like Tibby in *Howard's End* strike him as repulsively hard and cold. He is always girding against exclusiveness; he even criticises

South Hertfordshire, because it contains so many fenced-in gentlemen's parks. That human beings should be united with each other in love is to him the first need in life. The first fact about it, on the other hand, is that they are not so united. This contrast between what man wants in relation to his fellows, and what he gets is the outstanding feature of Mr. Forster's vision of the world.

He is not content, however, merely to record it. This is where his moralism shows itself. It is wrong as well as sad that people should be divided from each other. The wrong should be righted. Mr. Forster is deeply concerned to discover how this can be done. In his earlier books he seeks a remedy in a sort of Whitmanesque faith in Nature. The primitive, spontaneous, natural man does not feel cut off from his kind. But artificial divisions have made him so: divisions of class, convention, of nation. If man would put aside these false idols, erected by tradition and selfish wordliness, and yield himself uninhibitedly to the worship of the great God Pan, the great God Pan would save him. The people in these early books group themselves according as to how they react to this choice. On the one hand are the "natural" characters, Gino, Stephen Wonham, the Emersons; against them are ranged Mrs. Herriton and her daughter, the Pembroke family, Cecil Vyse, most of the visitors to the Pension Bertolini. Between them waver Philip Herriton, Ricky and Lucy Honeychurch. They waver partly from timidity; for to follow Pan needs courage. Pan and his followers can be rough and ruthless. But even their brutality, because it is uninhibited, clears the air and breaks down barriers; it is the sign of a genuine relationship. The

N

barriers, however, must be broken down by feeling, not intellect.   Philip in *Where Angels Fear to Tread* and Ansell in *The Longest Journey* fail at first to overcome their inhibitions because they strive to remove them by a deliberate intellectual process and not by yielding simply to the pressure of the instinctive movement of their hearts.

In his next book, *Howard's End*, Mr. Forster's interpretation of man's predicament is a little different. Once more we are presented with a division; the division between the humane, civilised individualistic Schlegels on the one hand and the efficient, Philistine, anti-individualistic Wilcoxes on the other.   Mutually attracted and repelled, they come into a conflict which results in disaster and impasse.   Though the Wilcoxes are vanquished, the rift between them and the Schlegels remains.   Once more, however, Nature steps in as saviour.   Only this time it is Nature symbolised less by Pan than by Ceres, the serene, unchanging mother of the earth and its children, whose spirit has been expressed earlier in the book by the august inarticulate figure of the first Mrs. Wilcox, and which continues to pervade the atmosphere of her house, Howard's End.   To Howard's End, Mr. Wilcox and Margaret Schlegel retire at the conclusion of the story, where, yielding themselves resignedly to the cycle of night and day, spring and autumn, death and birth, they find their differences slowly dissolved, their souls mysteriously healed and revived.

A Passage to India represents another modification of Mr. Forster's original attitude.   Here the division is between Indians and the English in India; midway between these opposing parties stand a tolerant, peace-loving group, Fielding, Mrs. Moore and Miss Quested. The crisis of the book comes when the last trio go on a picnic to the Marabar caves with the Hindu, Aziz. Suddenly their effort at friendship with him is frustrated; not by human agency this time, but by Nature, Nature appearing for the first time in Mr. Forster's works as a potentially malignant force. Some dangerous, hostile strain in the elemental constitution of things manifests itself in the caves, supernaturally, it would seem, affecting the characters. Mysteriously it exhales an atmosphere baleful and irresistible which, as she breathes it, turns Miss Quested into Aziz's enemy. The conclusion of the book, however, is not wholly pessimistic. In the strange last section, set significantly in a native state where Indian and English are not pitted one against the other, the surviving characters attend a religious festival, where the spirit of nature shows itself once more benignant. During the feast each one feels himself involuntarily lifted to a region of mystical bliss where human differences are resolved in a sense of the union of all creation. Only as long as it lasts though: in the final paragraphs of the book, once more back to common earth again, human divisions reveal themselves as unbridgeable as ever.

" 'Why can't we be friends now?' said the other, holding him affectionately. 'It's what I want. It's what you want.'

"But the horses didn't want it—they swerved apart; the earth didn't want it, sending up rocks through which riders must pass single file; the temples, the tank, the jail, the palace, the birds, the carrion, the Guest
N*

House, that came into view as they issued from the gap and saw Mau beneath: they didn't want it, they said in their hundred voices, 'No, not yet,' and the sky said, 'No, not there'."

We are left in a state of doubt. There is a passage earlier in the book in which Mr. Forster describes Fielding and Miss Quested at the end of one of their incessant conversations on the Indian problem.

"Perhaps life is a mystery, not a muddle. Perhaps the hundred Indias which fuss and squabble so tiresomely are one and the universe they mirror are one. They had not the apparatus of judging."

Their creator does not seem to have the apparatus either.

Such then is the vision of life presented in Mr. Forster's books. It is a complex one to incarnate in novel form; for it involves the fusion of such diverse elements. The drama is a realistic drama, a picture of every-day human life as Mr. Forster sees it. As such, it must give a convincing illusion of this every-day life. Yet since he is also out to express a moral and spiritual interpretation of experience, Mr. Forster has to make use of symbol and allegory. He has evolved a form specifically to solve this problem. His moral purpose is the basis of it. Not character or probability, but the thesis he wishes to expound determines the main lines of his plot's structure. But this structure is concealed beneath a closely woven fabric of realistic detail: and the one is still further assimilated to the other by a continuously running flow of comment—

moral, satirical, whimsical—addressed to the reader by the author. So that symbol and realistic description are alike conveyed to us in the same highly idiosyncratic tone of voice.

Certainly a very difficult kind of book to write successfully! Mr. Forster, however, brings an extraordinary accomplishment to his task. Mastery of form for one thing; not a detail in the scene or dialogue, however casual-seeming, but contributes to the general effect. And he tells a story as well as anyone who ever lived. Incident follows incident in a series of pictures, easy, vivid, economically drawn, and always, either unexpected in themselves or presented from a slightly unexpected angle, so that the reader's curiosity is kept quiveringly and delightfully astir. Sometimes, it is true, this unexpectedness becomes too much of a trick. In *The Longest Journey* for instance, too many people die suddenly: and Mr. Forster's way of announcing their deaths—every time with the same deliberate lack of emphasis or preparation—does seem an affectation. But how effective his unexpectedness can be, in its proper place. Look at the account of the street brawl in Florence in *The Room with a View*.

" 'Nothing ever happens to me,' she reflected, as she entered the Piazza Signoria and looked nonchalantly at its marvels, now fairly familiar to her. . . . Then something did happen. Two Italians by the Loggia had been bickering about a debt. 'Cinque lire,' they had cried, 'cinque lire!' They sparred at each other, and one of them was hit lightly upon the chest. He frowned; he bent towards Lucy with a look of interest, as if he

had an important message for her. He opened his lips
to deliver it, and a stream of red came out between
them and trickled down his unshaven chin. That was
all. A crowd rose out of the dusk. It hid this extraordinary man from her, and bore him away to the
fountain."

Narrative power, however, is not enough to make a
successful serious novelist. Novels are about people;
they live through their characters. Mr. Forster has an
acute insight into certain aspects of character. He is a
subtle observer of the actual movement of the human
mind: with microscopic exactness he traces and analyses
the blended course of thought and feeling and changing
mood behind a fragment of dialogue. Listen to Ronnie
and Miss Quested when they have just broken off
their engagement.

" 'We've been awfully British over it, but I suppose
that's all right.'

'As we are British, I suppose it is.'

'Anyhow we've not quarrelled, Ronny.'

'Oh, that would have been too absurd. Why should
we quarrel?'

'I think we shall keep friends.'

'I know we shall.'

'Quite so.'

"As soon as they had exchanged this admission, a
wave of relief passed through them both, and then
transformed itself into a wave of tenderness, and passed
back. They were softened by their own honesty, and
began to feel lonely and unwise. Experiences, not
character, divided them; they were not dissimilar,

as humans go; indeed, when compared with the people who stood nearest to them in point of space they became practically identical. The Bhil who was holding an officer's polo pony, the Eurasian who drove the Nawab Bahadur's car, the Nawab Bahadur himself, the Nawab Bahadur's debauched grandson—none would have examined a difficulty so frankly and coolly. The mere fact of examination caused it to diminish. Of course they were friends, and for ever.

" 'Do you know what the name of that green bird up above us is?' she asked, putting her shoulder rather nearer to his.

'Bee-eater.'

'Oh no, Ronny, it has red bars on its wings.'

'Parrot', he hazarded.

'Good gracious, no.'

"The bird in question dived into the dome of the tree. It was of no importance, yet they would have liked to identify it, it would somehow have solaced their hearts."

Mr. Forster's picture of mankind is brought to life by a hundred little strokes of nature, of penetrating observation into the characteristic complex of sentiment, impulse and motive implicit in apparently trivial acts and insignificant speeches; flickering qualms of conscience, unconscious self-deceptions, spontaneous betrayals of bias.

" 'Why not ask the Pleaders to the club?' Miss Quested persisted. 'Not allowed.' He was pleasant and patient, evidently understood why she did not understand. He implied that he had once been as she, though not for long."

Or to take another passage from *Howard's End*.

" 'Money pads the edges of things,' said Miss Schlegel. 'God help those who have none.' 'But this is something quite new!' said Mrs. Munt, who collected new ideas as a squirrel collects nuts, and was especially attracted by those that are portable."

These last two passages are humorous. Humour is the most sustained and unquestionable of all Mr. Forster's gifts; he brilliantly continues that delicate comedy tradition that descends through the English domestic novel from Jane Austen onwards; but adding to it a vagrant airy whimsicality all his own.

"Gathering that the wedding dress was on view and that a visit would be seemly, she went to Evie's room. All was hilarity here. Evie in a petticoat was dancing with one of the Anglo-Indian ladies, while the other was adoring yards of white satin. They screamed, they laughed, they sang, and the dog barked. Margaret screamed a little too, but without conviction. She could not feel that a wedding was so funny. Perhaps something was missing in her equipment."

The demure smile implicit in these curt, charming sentences is never absent from Mr. Forster's lips for long. Indeed, for all that the purpose of his books is so serious and their conclusions often so painful, he is essentially a comedian. Though he can be touched by

his characters' emotions, he never respects them as a
tragedian does; nor does he identify himself with them.
Always we are aware of the author standing a little
outside his drama, judging, criticising, observing, with
an irony sometimes bitter, more often sympathetic,
the hot, perplexed, undignified little bundles of hopes
and aspirations, fears and desires that he conceives
human beings to be. An incidental result of this is that
he draws most successfully types who naturally provoke
a smile; nervous, serious, comical maiden ladies like
Miss Bartlett and Miss Lavish; undignified, pathetic
mixtures of contradictory impulses like Aziz; comically
unselfconscious children of nature like Gino. On the
rare occasions when he attempts to portray a grander
and more dignified spirit—old Mr. Emerson in *The
Room with a View* for example—Mr. Forster is not so
convincing. We feel that at heart he does not believe
in dignity and is with difficulty restraining himself
from debunking it: indeed he can only avoid doing so
by becoming sentimental. Alas the comedian, grown
serious, turns all too often into a sentimentalist!

Not that there is any question of Mr. Forster being
only a comedian. Blended with his comic vein, and
equally characteristic of him, is his poetry. He has an
acute lyrical sensibility; to landscape, to music, and
more especially, to the imaginative charm of the exotic,
the Indian scene, the Italian scene. His response to
such things is less exclusively æsthetic than Virginia
Woolf's. Romantic association counts for more in it
than mere sensuous appeal to eye or ear. Always it
sets his imagination to work, embodying the emotion
it evokes in him in all manner of dreams and fanciful
figures.

"The great square was in shadow; the sunshine had come too late to strike it. Neptune was already unsubstantial in the twilight, half god, half ghost, and his fountain plashed dreamily to the men and satyrs who idled together on its marge. The Loggia showed as the triple entrance of a cave, wherein dwelt many a deity, shadowy, but immortal, looked forth upon the arrivals and departures of mankind. It was the hour of unreality —the hour, that is, when unfamiliar things are real. An older person at such an hour and in such a place might think that sufficient was happening to him, and rest content. Lucy desired more.

"She fixed her eyes wistfully on the tower of the palace, which rose out of the lower darkness like a pillar of roughened gold. It seemed no longer a tower, no longer supported by earth, but some unattainable treasure throbbing in the tranquil sky. Its brightness mesmerised her, still dancing before her eyes, when she bent them to the ground and started towards home."

Lovely as this passage is, it is not pitched so high as to be inconsistent with the comic spirit. Mr. Forster's poetry never is. The tone in which he speaks remains colloquial, the arabesques with which he decorates his vision are, as often as not, freaked with an elfish humour. "The sun rose high in its zenith, guided not by Phateon but by Apollo, competent, unswerving, divine." Thus he describes a beautiful autumn morning. But if it does not dissipate his comedy, Mr. Forster's poetry modifies it. He is a romantic comedian. He satirises from the standard not of common sense, but of uncommon sensibility. Behind the little group of precisely drawn Jane Austen figures, and making them look by contrast a trifle absurd, stretches a dreamy vista of turf and tree and filmy distance through which flit, scarcely seen, the insubstantial forms of faun and dryad.

It is an odd combination; and makes a complex impression on the imagination of the reader. Indeed the flavour of a Forster novel is eminently complex. The poet, the satirist and the moralist all contribute ingredients to it. In the space of one paragraph Mr. Forster can be wise and flippant, censorious and lyrical. It is this variety which gives his books their peculiar fascination. After reading one of his packed, live, iridescent pages, the work of most other authors seems obvious and monotone. For the concourse of so many streams—intelligence, fancy, observation, moral judgment—all flowing swift and high, sets the whole shimmering and foaming and frothing with an extraordinary and varied vitality. Every inch of surface is continuously animated by the play of mind: hardly a sentence but gives us a little shock of surprise and interest. And delight; for all the diverse elements are fused together in charming harmony by Mr. Forster's use of language. Style in the work of most novelists is of secondary importance. We read them for what they say, rather than how they say it. Mr. Forster's style is a chief instrument in the pleasure his books give. Like all the best styles it is an exact mirror of its author's mind and temperament. Not in any sense is it a grand style; there is no eloquence or burning passion in it. But it is infinitely sensitive, infinitely dexterous, infinitely graceful. In it, all his diverse qualities are to be seen deftly and fastidiously translated into his very choice of epithet, the very lilt and tempo of his light tuneful unpredictable rhythms. Nor does complexity ever obscure beauty. Mr. Forster is like a dancer who can execute the most complicated steps easily and without making a single ugly movement.

"Few things have been more beautiful than my notebook on the Deist Controversy as it fell downward through the waters of the Mediterranean. It dived, like a piece of black slate, but opened soon, disclosing leaves of pale green, which quivered into blue. Now it had vanished, now it was a piece of magical india-rubber stretching out to infinity, now it was a book again, but bigger than the book of all knowledge. It grew more fantastic as it reached the bottom, where a puff of sand welcomed it and obscured it from view. But it reappeared, quite sane though a little tremulous, lying decently open on its back, while unseen fingers fidgeted among its leaves."

With all these qualities Mr. Forster ought to be one of the most satisfactory of novelists. But, somehow this is not so. In spite of all their brilliance and all their charm his books leave an oddly ambiguous impression in the mind. Our pleasure in them is flawed: shot through by moments of disbelief, even of discomfort. The disbelief is largely due to a technical defect, almost inevitable considering the extreme difficulty of the task he has set himself. He does not, for all his art, always succeed in harmonising realism and symbolism. As his stories shift from one to the other, now and again we feel a jar. The symbolic episode is too improbable for the reader to maintain his illusion of everyday reality. To take an example;

Helen Schlegel's seduction of Leonard Bast in *Howard's
End*. The symbolic significance of the incident
is clear. The Wilcox point of view and the Schlegel
point of view have come into conflict over Bast; Helen
thinks that the Wilcoxes have ill-treated him. In
order therefore to demonstrate her defiant disapproval
of that whole social system of which the Wilcoxes are
pillars, she commits the most flagrant breach of its
conventions of which she can think; suddenly,
unpredictably, in the space apparently of a few hours,
she persuades Bast to become her lover. The only
trouble about the episode is that the reader cannot
believe a word of it. Neither party to the intrigue is in
love with the other; and Helen, for all her theoretically
emancipated views, has up till then been represented
as a respectable, serious Edwardian middle-class lady
without any unusual strength of sexual temperament
and surely incapable of setting about the seduction of
a timid young man of humble station with this breath-
taking speed and efficiency. Again, what are we to
make of the scene in *The Longest Journey* where Ricky,
hearing casually on a country walk that he possesses
an illegitimate brother, faints dead away. Once more
the symbolic intention is clear enough. The greatest
shock that can befall Ricky, hidebound as he is by
puritan convention, is to discover that the animal
passions from which he has been taught to shrink,
have already made themselves known, with very
practical results, in the life of his own parents. All the
same, it is not credible that a mature young man, even
in the virtuous days of good King Edward the Seventh,
should be so sensitive as actually to lose consciousness
at such a revelation.

The demands of his symbolic pattern also lead Mr. Forster astray by making him go outside his creative range; and to attempt character and experience too alien for him to be able to give it imaginative life. Consider the portrait of Stephen, the illegitimate brother in question. Stephen's function is to express that primitive virile paganism, some infusion of which is necessary for the salvation of Ricky's soul. Primitive virility, however, of any kind is remote from Mr. Forster's super-civilised spirit: with the result that Stephen is most unconvincing. He is credible as long as he is silent, tossing off a glass of beer at the public house, or silhouetted against the sky as he gallops on horse-back over the Wiltshire downs. But when he begins to speak, it is as Mr. Forster and his friends speak. Out of his rugged lips come the incongruous accents of a gentle Cambridge undergraduate, having a cosy heart-to-heart chat with a dear friend.

"The cloud descended lower. 'Come with me as a man,' said Stephen, already out in the mist. 'Not as a brother; who cares what people did years back? We're alive together, and the rest is cant. Here am I, Ricky, and there are you, a fair wreck. They've no use for you here—never had any, if the truth was known—and they've only made you beastly.' "

And the masculine George Emerson, breaking down Lucy's sexual inhibitions, addresses her in similar tones. All too often Mr. Forster's toughs turn out to be muffs under their skins.

As a matter of fact Mr. Forster is liable to go outside his range even when he is not impelled thither by the pressure of his symbolic pattern. This range is as

unusual as everything else about him. It is not confined
to a single social group like Hardy's peasants and Jane
Austen's county gentry. He can write equally about
dogs and bank clerks, English spinsters and Indian
students—as long as he confines himself to those sides
of their characters which he understands. There are
sides which he does not. His knowledge of human
nature is, as it were, patchy. Sometimes his plot takes
him on to patches outside his range. Then his picture
loses reality. This most frequently occurs when he
touches on those elemental human relations for which
he has so little instinctive feeling. The relation of
parent to child for instance; of Mrs. Moore to Ronnie
or Mrs. Honeychurch to Lucy. Mrs. Moore and Mrs.
Honeychurch are supposed to be fond of their children:
yet they show none of that instinctive identification of
themselves with them, that untiring preoccupation with
their interests and happiness which, however marred
by irritation or stupidity, is outstandingly characteristic
of the maternal relation. They behave to their children
like friendly aquaintances or, at best, friendly aunts.
More acutely still does Mr. Forster's deficiency appear
when he writes of the relations between the sexes. His
novels like most other novels involve engagements and
marriages. It is not unfair to say that hardly one of
them is credible. Margaret Schlegel and Mr. Wilcox,
Ronnie Moore and Miss Quested, Ricky and Caroline
Pembroke, Lucy and Cecil—what on earth, we ask
ourselves, has brought these incongruous pairs together?
They have not got a thought in common with one
another, nor is Mr. Forster able to account for their
connection by suggesting the impelling force of animal
passion. The feelings of the heroines are especially

unconvincing. Since women are more instinctive than men, they are a less fit subject for Mr. Forster. His heroines are not masculine, but they are strangely sexless; nervous, honest, unaware of their bodies, preoccupied with intellectual problems. It is impossible to imagine what they looked like, or to visualise them as being of any particular age.

The curious feeling of discomfort, however, which his books leave on the mind is due to a deeper cause; to a fundamental confusion in that moral vision which gives his books their perspective. His professed moral beliefs do not correspond to his instinctive moral feelings. Intellectually he is convinced that the divisions between human beings can be broken down by allowing the natural love of man for man to have free play, the elemental qualities common to humanity to express themselves; but in fact he himself can not convey the presence of these qualities. The differences between diverse types strike him so strongly that they scarcely seem beings of the same species. There is in his world no common emotional plane on which Ricky and the Pembrokes, Schlegels and Wilcoxes find their individual differences sunk in common humanity. We do feel the conflict between Englishman and High-lander in Scott's *Two Drovers* to be a tragic one, because Scott makes us so vividly aware that, in spite of the differences engendered in them by national tradition, they are in a sense brothers; and, as such, should be able to live in perfect harmony with each other. In *A Passage to India* Indians and English appear almost as different as cats and dogs; so that there is no inner clash within the breasts of each strong enough to produce tragic tension. Further, though Mr. Forster always preaches tolerance and sympathy, involuntarily he reveals himself as not particularly sympathetic or tolerant. It is all very well to tell us that the Pembrokes in *The Longest Journey* were in the wrong because they were unable to enter into any point of view but their own. What sign of sympathy does Mr. Forster show of entering into their point of view? They are portrayed wholly and only as monsters of hardness and stupidity. So in a less degree with the Wilcox family in *Howard's End*. It is a basic postulate of his drama that the Wilcoxes possessed certain virtues which the Schlegels admired and lacked; good sense, practical ability and a straightforward kindness that made them useful to society. There is in consequence something to be said on both sides in the Wilcox-Schlegel conflict. Mr. Forster, however, does not say it. He dislikes the Wilcox vices so much that he cannot do any effective justice to their virtues. The Wilcoxes are portrayed as so insensitive and complacent and materialistic that the reader cannot understand how the Schlegels, or any other civilised person, tolerated their company for an hour. The question is not whether Mr. Forster is or is not justified in disliking the Wilcox type. An author is at liberty to dislike whom he feels inclined. And we— whatever our personal feelings—must, while receiving the hospitality of his world, fall in with his inclinations. But Mr. Forster has not the courage of his dislikes. He errs in trying to persuade us that he is describing something with sympathetic impartiality, when in fact he is doing nothing of the kind. Told to feel one thing and forced to feel another, the reader finds his pleasure checked by an involuntary impulse of protesting irritation.

A similar gap between intention and performance impairs the effect of his moments of ecstasy; those passages when the characters, under the influence of Pan or Ceres or Krishna or whatever deity it may be by which Mr. Forster symbolises the healing spiritual force of the natural universe, feel their souls released, to soar upwards into rapturous union with something greater than themselves; the bathing scene in *A Room with a View*, the laughing fight between Ansell and Stephen in *The Longest Journey*, the festival at the end of *A Passage to India*. The first two passages fail partly because the incidents they describe are not strong enough to carry the weight of significance Mr. Forster attaches to them. The deep-seated inhibitions of a lifetime are surely not to be removed by an hour's schoolboy ragging or even by bathing naked in company. Salvation by romps is not a credible concept. But perhaps Mr. Forster does not at heart think it is either. These scenes fail more fundamentally because they do not communicate the emotion the characters are supposed to be feeling; so that we doubt if in fact the author believed that they did. He would like to, but that is a different thing. The Festival in *A Passage to India* is far better. The forces of nature in *A Passage to India*—mysterious, half-malevolent, half-benignant—are much more plausibly conceived. Indeed the festival is a wonderful flight of fancy, shimmering with its author's typical blend of romantic imagination and elfin comedy. All the same, Mr. Forster hardly succeeds in conveying to us that sense of mystical exaltation which he appears to have in mind. Again, rightly or not, we are unconvinced that he has himself experienced it. Rather he seems to be talking on hearsay;

to be weaving a day-dream of what he would like to be
true, though he is not sure it is. Hearsay and wish-
fulfilment dreams are not enough to convince us of the
truth of a mystical vision.

No wonder Mr. Forster leaves his readers a little
uncomfortable! This inability to achieve a consistent
moral relation to his subject-matter means that the
world of his creation is fundamentally unstable. For,
unluckily, that world rests on moral foundations; it is
the expression of his moral vision. If that vision is
incoherent, if those foundations are insecure, so also
is the building that rests on them. We move through it
entranced but uneasy; for we are, half consciously,
aware that at any moment the whole delicate structure
may come tumbling about our ears.